The Resilience of Networked Infrastructure Systems

Analysis and Measurement

SYSTEMS RESEARCH SERIES

Series Editor: Dinesh Verma *(Stevens Inst. of Technology, USA)*

Published:

Systems Research Series — Vol. 3

The Resilience of Networked Infrastructure Systems

Analysis and Measurement

Mayada Omer

Stevens Institute of Technology, USA

 **World Scientific**

NEW JERSEY · LONDON · SINGAPORE · BEIJING · SHANGHAI · HONG KONG · TAIPEI · CHENNAI

Published by

World Scientific Publishing Co. Pte. Ltd.

5 Toh Tuck Link, Singapore 596224

USA office: 27 Warren Street, Suite 401-402, Hackensack, NJ 07601

UK office: 57 Shelton Street, Covent Garden, London WC2H 9HE

Library of Congress Cataloging-in-Publication Data
Omer, Mayada.
    The resilience of networked infrastructure systems / Mayada Omer, Stevens Institute of Technology, USA.
        pages cm -- (Systems research series ; 3)
        Includes bibliographical references and index.
        ISBN 978-9814452816 (alk. paper)
    1. Reliability (Engineering) 2. Infrastructure (Economics) 3. Computer networks--Reliability.
I. Title.
    TA169.O44 2013
    003'.72--dc23

                                                                    2013019825

British Library Cataloguing-in-Publication Data
A catalogue record for this book is available from the British Library.

In-house Editor: Amanda Yun

Printed in Singapore

Dedication

I dedicate this thesis to my husband, Martin Ostermayr, and to my parents, Zeinab Mahmoud and Mohamed Ibrahim Ali Omer.

Dedication

Acknowledgments

Pursuing a full-time PhD in Systems Engineering was an unexpected deviation from my regular line of work. Although it was a challenging endeavor, working on this research was a pleasurable experience that I owe to the support of my committee members, my family and friends.

My thanks and gratitude goes to my advisor Dr Roshanak Nilchiani for offering me the opportunity to work on this topic, and for the valuable advice that enabled me to complete the dissertation. It was an honor and a pleasure to have Dr Ali Mostashari as my co-advisor, he has been truly inspirational. I would also like to thank Dr Thomas Wakeman and Dr Brian Sauser for their guidance that broadened the horizon of my research.

I am blessed with an amazing family who mean the world to me. My partner in life, Martin, the joy of my life, Yassin, my mother, Zeinab Mahmoud, my father, Mohamed Ibrahim Ali Omer, my siblings, Rahab, Hisham, Rasha and Selma, my nephew and niece, Iyaas and Sariyah, and my in-laws, Anneliese and Hermann Ostermayr.

Martin, you have been my anchor throughout the whole process; this PhD would not have been possible without you. I owe everything to mum and dad who taught us to take the challenges of life on our stride and to reach for what we thought was unachievable. Thanks dad, for stepping outside of the realm of your medical jargon and proofreading my dissertation. My siblings have always been there for me when I needed them; may we always be there for each other.

I would also like to thank my dear friend, Ana-Lisbeth Concho, for running errands for me at Stevens when I could not be there myself. Thanks Lisbeth for your friendship.

    This material is based upon work supported by the U.S. Department of Homeland Security under Grant Award Number 2008-ST-061-ML0002.

Disclaimer

The views and conclusions contained in this work are those of the author and should not be interpreted as necessarily representing the official policies, either expressed or implied, of the U.S. Department of Homeland Security.

Abstract

For natural and man-made systems, change, disruptive events and disasters occur on a frequent basis. Every now and then, major catastrophes can leave a large-scale critical infrastructure system devastated, defenseless or nonoperational. Examples of such devastating events are: Hurricane Katrina in 2005 and the September 11 attacks in 2001; these events have awakened an interest in infrastructure resilience.

As a result, there has been a significant emphasis on understanding the concept of resilience and how it can be implemented in large-scale infrastructure systems. There have been several efforts focusing on developing guidelines, frameworks and methodologies to help understand the resilience of specific systems, as well as risk-mitigating solutions. However, little effort has gone into developing a methodology based on the systems perspective that incorporates quantitative metrics and techniques to measure the value of infrastructure resilience.

This research attempts to fill this gap by proposing the Networked Infrastructure Resilience Assessment (NIRA) framework, through which the resilience of the system can be measured quantitatively by assessing the impact of disruptions on the performance measures of the system. The framework consists of a series of steps that include the identification of the system's boundary, assessment of the system's resilience metrics, and the identification and evaluation of appropriate resilience-enabling schemes.

The ability of the proposed framework in assessing resilience across a wide variety of networked infrastructure systems is demonstrated by applying the framework to five case studies representing four different types of critical infrastructure systems. The case studies probe the resilience of the following infrastructure systems in the face of specific disruptive events: telecommunication, transportation, maritime transportation and organizational networks.

Contents

Chapter 1

Introduction

It was a sunny September day when a tremendous explosion rang out across Manhattan. The North Tower of the World Trade Center burst into flames as hijackers crashed American Airlines Flight 11 into the building symbolizing the power of the United States of America. Minutes later, as the chaos spread among disbelieving spectators, United Airlines Flight 175 smashed into the South Tower, setting it aflame. The Twin Towers burned for almost an hour before collapsing into a heap of rubble and twisted metal, killing more than 2,600 people (Kean *et al.* 2010).

Fig. 1.1. Seconds after the second plane crashed into the South Tower of the World Trade Center. Source: http://ginacobb.typepad.com.

The September 11 attacks rocked the nation and indeed the whole world. The destruction left behind an abyss of fear and anger, and many wondering whether the incident could have been avoided and whether more could have been done to minimize the consequences. A few years later, in 2005, the devastation wrought by Hurricane Katarina highlighted the fragility of the current infrastructure systems even further.

In the wake of these catastrophic events, the U.S. Department of Homeland Security (DHS) initiated the Critical Infrastructure Protection (CIP) program. The critical infrastructure systems include telecommunications, electrical power systems, gas and oil, banking and finance, transportation, water supply systems, and government and emergency services. They are critical because they are vital for our everyday lives and are essential for the functioning of society and the economy.

The goal of the CIP program is to protect these infrastructure systems, and consequently the people who use them, from man-made and natural disasters by increasing security (McCarthy 2007). However, the focus is slowly shifting from CIP to Critical Infrastructure Resilience (CIR), since CIP does not address all aspects of securing the nation's critical infrastructure.

Resilient infrastructures are not only secure; they are also able to "bounce back" after severe disruptions. They are able to absorb shock and recover from disruptions so that normal levels of service delivery can resume. Implementing resilience in infrastructure systems improves their ability to cope in the face of disruptions while continuing to deliver the required value delivery of the system.

Under the Obama administration, the Department of Homeland Security and other sector partners are implementing the National Infrastructure Protection Plan (NIPP) (NIPP 2009), which focuses on infrastructure resilience. The goal of this plan is to

> ... build a safer, more secure, and **more resilient** America by preventing, deterring, neutralizing, or mitigating the effects of deliberate efforts by terrorists to destroy, incapacitate, or exploit elements of our Nation's CIKR[1] and to strengthen national preparedness, timely response, and rapid recovery of CIKR in the event of an attack, natural disaster, or other emergency.

---

[1]CIKR: Critical Infrastructure and Key Resources

Infrastructure resilience is not limited to individual nations; it is an issue that concerns the global community. While catastrophes such as earthquakes impact local communities only, disruptions such as those caused by the Iceland volcano ash cloud in April 2010 created havoc for global air travel for several weeks.

With efforts focused on creating resilience in infrastructure systems, there is a critical need to develop measures and metrics of infrastructure resilience. While a significant amount of effort has been focused on developing frameworks and guidelines that help to understand some aspects of resilience in systems and the factors influencing infrastructure resilience, little effort has gone into developing quantitative metrics through which the infrastructure resilience can be measured.

The goal of this work is to propose a framework through which resilience metrics for infrastructure systems can be defined and evaluated. The suggested metrics will provide insight into the current state of the system's resilience and can be used as a benchmark to improve the system's resilience.

The primary focus and scope of this research are physical networked infrastructure systems such as water, transportation, telecommunication and power systems. These infrastructure systems (shown in Fig. 1.2) provide services based on the physical infrastructures. They are considered to be lifeline systems, since they link metropolitan areas and communities and provide basic facilities that are vital for the growth of local, regional and national economies (NRC 2009).

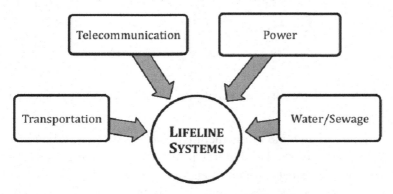

Fig. 1.2. Lifeline infrastructure systems.

1.1 Need for Resilience in Infrastructure Systems

Even in a peaceful, perfect world devoid of malicious terrorist acts, other factors such as weather events, aging equipment and inadequate maintenance as well as unforeseeable accidents will continue to assault infrastructure systems (Little 2002).

By their very nature, infrastructure systems do not exist in isolation; they are interdependent and can therefore influence one another. These interdependencies are complex and not easily understood. Figure 1.3 shows some of the interdependencies that exist between service infrastructures.

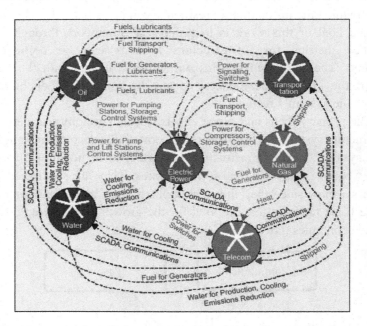

Fig. 1.3. An example of the complexity of interdependency interactions. Source: Rinaldi *et al.* (2001).

A failure in any one infrastructure could result in cascading failures in other infrastructures. The failures propagate from one element to the next and may have catastrophic consequences. Building resilience into infrastructures prepares the system for mitigating disasters and hence reduces the losses incurred by service disruption.

The September 11 attacks are a typical example of catastrophic failures due to interdependencies. The water mains servicing the World Trade Center (WTC) were ruptured due to the collapse of the towers; this resulted in a decrease in the water pressure around the WTC complex, which in turn impaired fire fighters. The Verizon cable vault was flooded because of the ruptured pipes, and as a result Verizon lost 200,000 voice lines, 100,000 private branch exchange lines, 4.4 million data circuits, and 11 cell sites, which affected 14,000 business and 20,000 residential customers (O'Rourke 2007).

Another example is the loss of electrical power following Hurricane Katrina, which in turn affected the operation of a crude oil refinery. This resulted in a failure to deliver 1.4 million barrels per day of crude oil—about 10 percent of the U.S. supply. It took some 17 days to restore the pipeline (O'Rourke 2007).

This work will not address the disruptions due the interdependencies between infrastructure systems. However, the interdependencies stress the importance of incorporating resilience, which begins with a careful assessment of the current state of infrastructure resilience.

1.2 Problem Statement

A disruption in any of the infrastructure systems will potentially cause substantial losses in other infrastructures since these systems are interdependent. It is therefore crucial to make the infrastructures less susceptible to disruptions, and to improve their ability to recover with minimum losses; that is, to create resilience in infrastructure systems.

Resilience metrics are required to provide insight into the current resilience of the system. The metrics provide stakeholders with the opportunity to determine the amount of resilience that is incorporated in the system, and to evaluate the improvement of the system's resilience after the implementation of resilience schemes. The metrics are also an effective tool for comparing and evaluating the different resilience schemes that enhance the system's resilience.

1.3 Research Question

The research question for this work is the following: *How can the resilience of networked infrastructure systems be measured?*

1.4 Research Hypothesis and Its Implications

Given the problem statement, the hypothesis of this research is as follows:

> *The resilience of a networked infrastructure system in the face of any set of disruptions to its link/node physical capacities can be measured by assessing their respective impacts on the infrastructure's key performance metrics.*

The following are the important implications of this hypothesis, if it is validated:

(i)   The resilience of a system depends on the type (node or link-level) and magnitude of the disruptions to the network (degree of capacity loss) of the disruptions to the network.

(ii)   The resilience of a system consists of a set of metrics that measure the impact of any disruption to the network on the performance measures.

(iii) Based on the above, it is possible to develop a general network-based modeling framework that can be applied to a variety of networked infrastructure systems.

1.5 Hypothesis Validation

In order to validate the hypothesis, we will develop a framework in which the infrastructure system is represented by a network model. The framework will provide a methodology, and acts as a guideline for measuring the impact of disruptions on the performance measures of the infrastructure system. Our hypothesis is validated if the impact of disruptions is indeed measurable by the changes in the key performance of the system.

1.6 Research Approach

The primary foci of this research are the "lifeline systems"; these are the infrastructure systems that are vital for everyday life. These infrastructure systems provide services based on the physical systems. They are also known as "network industries" because they can be represented as a series of nodes that are interconnected by links.

The Networked Infrastructure Resilience Assessment (NIRA) framework is suggested to evaluate the resilience of different infrastructure systems. The framework is also applicable to enterprise systems, which can also be viewed as a network. The framework is made up of several steps that help decision makers to

- determine the most critical and vulnerable segments in the network,
- identify the resilience metrics,
- analytically quantify the resilience metrics,
- assess the effectiveness of the proposed resilience enhancement schemes, and
- evaluate the benefits of the different resilience enhancement schemes using decision trees and cost–benefit analysis.

1.7 Research Contribution

A significant amount of effort has gone into defining resilience and ways to achieve resilience in infrastructure systems at an abstract level. However, little effort has gone into developing metrics that quantify the resilience of infrastructure systems. Additionally, many resilience-enabling schemes have been proposed with a view to improving the resilience of infrastructures. However, they have not been presented in a manner that will help decision makers assess the resilience of infrastructure systems and evaluate the effectiveness of the resilience-enabling options.

This research introduces a novel systems-oriented approach for measuring and evaluating the resilience of all types of physical networked infrastructure systems. The anticipated research contributions are as follows:

(i) To propose a single framework for measuring the resilience of infrastructure systems that will help stakeholders assess the system's current resilience.

   – The framework proposes modeling infrastructure systems mathematically, and applying the most suitable mathematical modeling techniques for the system under study (such as network flow analysis or systems dynamics).

   – The steps of the framework can be customized and applied to all types of networked physical infrastructure systems (such as transportation, telecommunications, power, etc.).

(ii) To measure the resilience of the system via a set of quantitative metrics that are based on the performance measures of the system.

(iii) To offer a comprehensive overview of resilience-enabling schemes.

   – The resilience schemes are focused on improving the two aspects of a resilient system: vulnerability and adaptive capacity.

   – The resilience schemes help decision makers identify the capabilities present in their own systems and how they can be combined to improve the resilience of the system.

(iv) To aid the stakeholders in evaluating the proposed resilience-enhancing schemes and in choosing between them using decision analysis tools and cash flow theory.

1.8 Research Assumptions

Conducting resilience research entails making several assumptions about how to model the system as a network and the analysis techniques for quantitatively assessing the resilience of the system. The assumptions of this research are as follows:

• Physical infrastructure systems can be modeled as networks that consist of nodes and links. Using the network model, it is possible to apply system-modeling techniques such as network flow analysis and system dynamics in order to predict the behavior of the systems under normal operating conditions and under disruptive scenarios.

Organizational networks that make up the organizational layer of infrastructure systems can be modeled and analyzed using well-established social network analysis tools.

• Resilience deals with the ability of the system to cope with disruptions. Therefore, it is assumed that disruptions manifest themselves in the form of capacity reduction of the links and/or nodes of the system's network model.

• The benefits of the proposed resilience schemes can be evaluated using decision analysis tools and cash flow theory.

1.9 Dissertation Structure

This book comprises of 10 chapters, as shown in Fig. 1.4. The following gives a brief description of each chapter.

Chapter 1 is an introduction to the research topic. Chapter 2 is a review of the relevant resilience literature; It offers an introduction on what resilience means for systems, why we need resilience, and the elements of resilience. The chapter also includes a review of the literature on what resilience means for enterprises and organizations.

In Chap. 3, the concept of resilience is compared to other system properties — namely, reliability, robustness, flexibility and agility. Chapter 4 is a comprehensive overview of resilience-enabling schemes that improve the resilience of infrastructure systems. The schemes are categorized into schemes that reduce the vulnerability of the system and schemes that increase the adaptive capacity.

The Networked Infrastructure Resilience Assessment Framework (NIRA) is presented in Chap. 5. The basic structure of the framework consists of six steps that are applicable to all networked infrastructure systems. It should be noted that the details of every step differ according to the type of infrastructure system under assessment.

A series of case studies demonstrating the application of the NIRA framework to a variety of networked infrastructure systems will be presented in Chaps. 6–9. The included case studies are as follows:

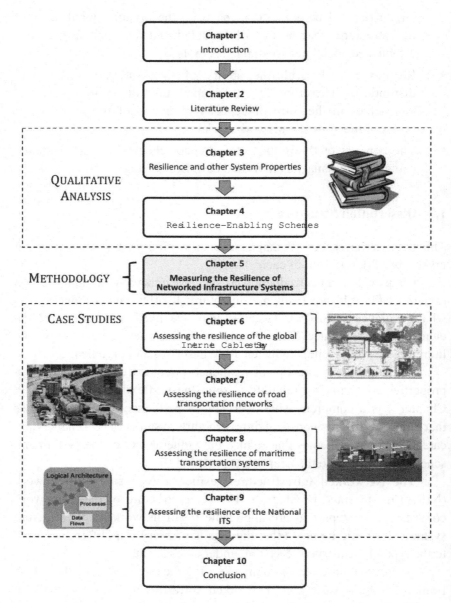

Fig. 1.4. Book outline.

- Assessing the resilience of the global internet infrastructure system
- Assessing the resilience of regional transportation networks. The case studies include:
  - The Boston–New York City road network
  - Manhattan's points of entry
- Assessing the resilience of maritime transportation systems (MTS)
- Assessing the resilience of the National Intelligent Transportation System

The conclusions are presented in Chap. 10; the chapter includes a summary of the book, contributions, research validation and the direction of future research.

Chapter 2

Literature Review

This chapter gives an overview of the various definitions of resilience for different systems and a brief description of the interpretations of resilience in the various disciplines. The chapter also covers the types of disruptions that create the need for implementing resilience in systems and the methodologies and metrics that have been used to assess resilience to date. Additionally, the elements of resilience upon which this book is based are introduced. Later on in the chapter, the main factors that contribute towards achieving resilience in organizations are summarized. The chapter concludes with an overview of the relationship between resilience and risk management as detailed in the literature.

2.1 Resilience Definitions

The term resilience comes from the Latin word *resilíre*, meaning "to leap back." Resilience in systems extends this definition to mean the ability of systems to "bounce back" after a disturbance has occurred. Many efforts have gone into defining and characterizing resilience, some of these definitions are summarized in the following paragraphs.

Folke *et al.* (2002) defines resilience as the capacity of the system to absorb disturbance and reorganize while undergoing change so as to retain the same function, structure, identity and feedbacks. Dalizell and McManus (2004) state that resilience describes the overarching goal of a system to continue to function to the fullest possible extent in the face of stress to achieve its purpose. Rose and Liao (2005) present a similar definition for systems resilience; they define resilience to be the ability of the system to apply adaptive responses in the face of disruptions in order to avoid potential losses.

Andersson (2006) views resilience as the ability of an actor, in the face of natural hazards, to cope with or adapt to hazard stress. He also mentions that the resilience is influenced by the proactive measures taken as a preparation for the hazard and the reactive measures in response to a hazard.

Fiksel (2003) defines a resilient system as a system that has the ability to return to a stable equilibrium state after a perturbation.

Bruneau *et al.* (2003) define a resilient system as one that has reduced failure probability, reduced consequences of failures, and reduced time to recovery. They also defined robustness, redundancy, resourcefulness and rapidity to be properties of resilient systems. Recent efforts by Reed *et al.* (2009) follow in these footsteps and identify quality as the capacity of the infrastructure. They define robustness to be the ratio of the lost capacity of the system as a result of a disruptive event to the capacity of a fully functioning structural system, and rapidity to be the measure of rapidity of recovery.

Pavard *et al.* (2006) define resilient systems to be those capable of maintaining a constant output value level when the system suffers from a perturbation.

The counterpart of resilience is brittleness. A resilient system is able to adapt to the shock and contain it; a brittle system, on the other hand, lacks the ability to adapt and transmits exogenous shocks (Wears and Perry 2008).

2.2 Resilience in Different Disciplines

The concept of resilience existed long before it was adopted for engineering systems. It was first introduced by Holling in 1973 (Holling 1973) for ecological systems. He defined the resilience of ecological systems to be "*the measure of the persistence of systems and their ability to absorb change and disturbance and still maintain the same relationship between populations or stat variables*"; that is, how far the system can be perturbed without shifting to a different regime. More resilient systems can absorb a larger amount of disturbance before shifting into a new regime (Walker *et al.* 2006).

Holling (1996) describes two views of resilience. The first is engineering resilience, which concentrates on the stability near an equilibrium steady state. It is measured through the resistance to disturbance and the speed of return to the steady state; more resilient systems have more than one equilibrium state. The second is ecological resilience, where the conditions are not at an equilibrium steady state. Here, the resilience is measured by the magnitude of disturbance that can be absorbed before the system changes its structure. Sugden (2001) relates the resilience of an ecosystem to recovery. He states that the resilience of an ecosystem is the extent to which the system can recover if an alien species is introduced to the system and then removed.

In psychology, resilience is the ability of an individual to withstand stresses and to bounce back or recover from traumatic situations; an example of a particularly resilient individual is Nelson Mandela, who went on to lead a country after years of solitary captivity (Neill 2006).

In materials science, resilience is the ability of the material to absorb energy when deformed elastically and to return to its original form when unloaded. It is represented by the area under the curve in the elastic region of the stress–strain diagram.

In business organizations, resilience is an issue of great importance since business disruptions can be fatal to an organization. Understanding and improving the resilience of the system entails looking into the interdependencies within and across organizations (Goble *et al.* 2002).

Figure 2.1 shows the resilience in different disciplines found in the literature.

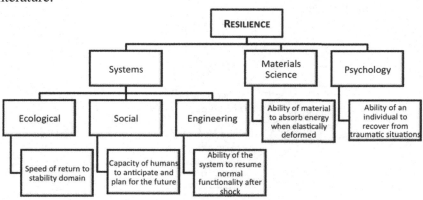

Fig. 2.1. Resilience in different disciplines.

2.3 Resilience and Disruptions (Shocks)

The primary factor for implementing resilience in systems is to improve the reaction of the system after the occurrence of disruptions or system shocks and improve its ability to resume functionality. The following sections will introduce the main factors that cause disruptions in infrastructure systems and the typical disruption profile that describes the state of the infrastructure system following a disruption.

2.3.1 *Categories of potential disruptions to systems*

Disruptions can be caused by various sources of threats. The level of resilience required by a system depends on the potential level of damage that may result from disruptions. Sources of disruptions have been grouped by Mansouri *et al.* (2009b) into the following (see Fig. 2.2):

- **Human Factors** — Disruptions caused by humans operating or using the system, such as malicious attacks or accidental disruptions as a result of human error.
- **Natural Factors** — Disruptions due to damage caused by nature, such as hurricanes and floods.
- **Organizational Factors** — Events that occur at the organizational level, such as a workers strike.
- **Technical Factors** — Failures in system components, such as when equipment is faulty.

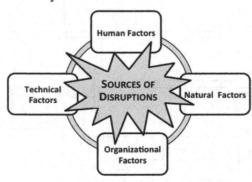

Fig. 2.2. Sources of disruptions. Adapted from Mansouri *et al.* (2009b).

Disruptions have been categorized by Westrum (2006) to be caused by regular and irregular threats. Regular threats occur frequently and these can be managed by preparing the systems to execute a standard response to overcome disruptions. Regular threats are predictable on a probabilistic basis, such as via statistical models, which are often used for estimating the likelihood of occurrence as well as the magnitude of natural disasters.

Most systems are designed according to system safety analysis guidelines that prepare the system to recover from predictable disruptions. Irregular threats are one-off events; predicting these types of disruptions is difficult, and in some cases, impossible. In general, whereas unpredictable disruptions may belong to any of the four categories, human disruptions are a little harder to predict than other sources of disruptions (Jackson 2009).

2.3.2 *Disruption profile*

When disaster strikes, the profile of the disruption on an infrastructure will typically have eight phases, as shown in Fig. 2.3 (Sheffi 2005).

The first phase, "Preparation," indicates how well the system is prepared against threats. This stage will include proactive resilience measures that reduce the damage of predictable events. Unforeseen threats could lead to a higher degree of damage.

The second phase, the "Disruptive Event," is the moment when the disruption occurs, followed by the "First Response," during which the initial damage is attended to. An example of such a response is providing first aid if there were human casualties. At the same time, the recovery preparation takes place during this stage, aiming to bring the system back to its normal state. The full impact of the disruption is often not felt immediately; it typically takes a certain amount of time for the full extent of the damage to be felt. The severity of the disruptive event dictates how long it will take the system to recover. In some cases, it is not possible to recover completely from the disruption.

The purpose of implementing resilience is to change the appearance of the disruptive profile by reducing the area between the dotted line representing the normal performance of the system and the dip, illustrated by the solid line, reflecting the impact of the disruptive event on the performance.

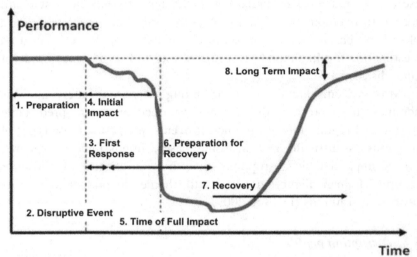

Fig. 2.3. Disruptive event profile. Source: Sheffi (2005).

2.4 Methodologies for Characterizing Resilience

Bruneau and Reinhorn (2007) defined the following four attributes to be dimensions of a resilient system:

- *Robustness* — the strength of a system and its elements to withstand a disruption

- *Redundancy* — the extent the system and its elements have substitutes to continue functioning after a disruptive event

- *Resourcefulness* — the capacity of the system to identify, prioritize and apply resources in the face of a disruption

- *Rapidity* — the capacity to meet priorities and achieve goals to limit loss and thwart future disruptions

Fiksel (2003) characterizes a resilient system as having multiple equilibrium points, and more resilient systems as having more equilibrium points. Figure 2.4 illustrates the different system states. The first curve shows a resistant system, which is able to recover rapidly from a small perturbation but may not survive a large perturbation. The second curve shows a resilient system that can operate across a broad spectrum and is able to survive large perturbations. The third system is the most resilient as it has multiple equilibrium states. This type of system is able to continue operation after a large perturbation by having multiple equilibrium states achievable through a structural change.

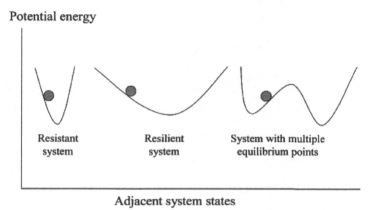

Fig. 2.4. Adjacent system states. Source: Fiksel (2003).

Similar concepts that define the state of resilience in systems were proposed by Walker *et al.* (2004):

- *Latitude* — the amount by which the system can change before it loses its ability to recover
- *Resistance* — the ease of changing the system
- *Precariousness* — how close the system is to its threshold

The benefits of implementing resilience in systems are seen after the occurrence of disruptions; these benefits are intensified based on the measures taken before the occurrence of the disruptive events. Richards *et al.* (2007) identify two phases, of resilience — namely, the anticipation/avoidance phase, and the survival/recovery phase. In the anticipation/avoidance phase, stakeholders need to identify foreseen and emergent vulnerabilities in order to take action that avoids or limits dangers (Pommerening 2007). The survival/recovery phase entails an adaptation to disruptions while maintaining operations.

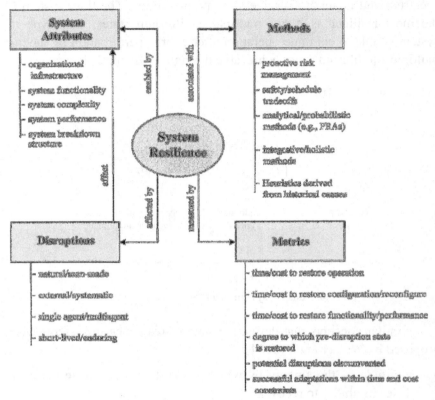

Fig. 2.5. Conceptual framework for resilience engineering.
Source: Madni and Jackson (2009).

Madni and Jackson (2009) have defined the pillars of resilience as: disruptions, systems attributes, methods, and metrics. The conceptual framework for the pillars of resilience is shown in Fig. 2.5.

The disruptions that can assault infrastructure systems result in a deterioration of the attributes that define the functionality of the infrastructure system. Traditional methods, such as risk and safety assessments, aid decision makers in making effective production/safety tradeoffs. However, metrics provide insight into various time and cost of restoration efforts, and how well the system responds to them.

2.5 Resilience Measurement Approaches

Holling introduced the concept of resilience in systems in 1973 (Holling 1973), but there was little motivation in quantitatively assessing resilience in the years prior to the September 11, 2001. Since the attacks, infrastructure resilience has become a topic of increasing interest. The following sections will review some of the resilience metrics that have been proposed for infrastructure systems.

2.5.1 *Infrastructure resilience metrics*

Bruneau and Reinhorn (2007) proposed a metric for measuring the seismic resilience of infrastructure systems. Their metric assumes a degradation of the quality of the infrastructure from 100 percent following an earthquake. The graph in Fig. 2.6 shows that if the time of occurrence of the disruptive event is t_0 and recovery is achieved at time t_1, the resilience can be measured as the time to recovery. This relationship is expressed in Eq. (2.1):

$$R = \int_{t_0}^{t_1} \left[100 - Q(t)\right] dt ,\qquad (2.1)$$

where R is the infrastructure resilience, $Q(t)$ is the quality of the infrastructure system, t_0 is the time of occurrence of the disruptive event, and t_1 marks the end of the recovery and restoration efforts.

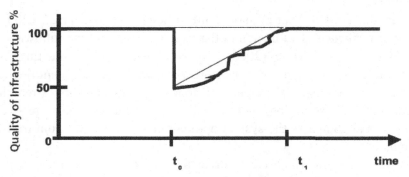

Fig. 2.6. Schematic representation of the seismic resilience concept. Source: Bruneau *et al.* (2003).

The "resilience triangle" in Fig. 2.6 represents the loss of functionality from damage and disruption, as well as the pattern of restoration and recovery over time. Although Bruneau and Reinhorn's efforts focus primarily on seismic resilience, their proposed metric can be tailored for any type of threat.

Reed *et al.* (2009) use this definition of resilience and identify the quality of the infrastructure as the infrastructure capacity. Infrastructure systems are interdependent by nature. Their research captures the interdependencies between the infrastructures through a linear function, although they state that a second-order trend might be more appropriate.

Attoh–Okine *et al.* (2009) propose the use of belief functions for measuring the resilience index of interdependent urban infrastructure systems.

Other efforts in defining resilience metrics for networked infrastructure systems include the methodology outlined by Garbin and Shortle (2007) where resilience metrics are the percentage of nodes or links damaged in the network versus the network performance.

2.5.2 *Service infrastructures resilience metrics*

Resilience metrics have also been defined for service infrastructures. Considering power infrastructures, Shinozuka *et al.* (2004) measure the resilience of power systems in terms of speed of restoration and repair efficiency. Chang and Chamberlin (2005) measure resilience in terms of economic loss.

In the field of transportation infrastructure, Werner *et al.* (2005) measure resilience as a function of the increase in travel time following a disruption. Murray-Tuite (2006) proposes metrics for evaluating 10 components of transport infrastructure resilience that she identifies as redundancy, diversity, efficiency, autonomous components, strength, adaptability, collaboration, mobility, safety, and the ability to recover quickly, and compares the system optimum and user equilibrium traffic assignments.

Heaslip *et al.* (2009) categorize the metrics with regards to the transportation infrastructure under individual resilience, community resilience, economic resilience, and recovery metrics; each metric is evaluated as a combination of several indices that describe each metric.

Considering telecommunications infrastructure, specifically the Internet, Cohen *et al.* (2001) study the tolerance of the Net to intentional attack; the proposed resilience metric being a measurement of the number of sites needed for the disintegration of the network. Dolev *et al.* (2006) explore the resilience of the Internet at the autonomous system level. They propose resilience metrics derived from network properties such as the number of connected nodes in the network. Omer *et al.* (2009) propose a metric for the global transoceanic telecommunications network as the ratio of the value delivery of a network after a disruption to the value delivery before a disruption — the value delivery being identified as the amount of data transferred across the cables.

2.6 Elements of Resilience

The elements of resilience are the elements that need to be addressed in order to achieve resilience. Achieving resilience in systems is addressed in terms of vulnerability and adaptive capacity. Making a system less vulnerable and increasing its adaptive capacity results in a more resilient system. This relationship is illustrated in Fig. 2.7.

The following sections establish the linkages of vulnerability and adaptive capacity to resilience.

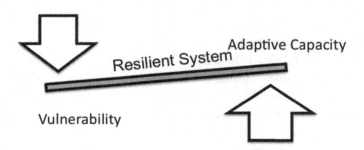

Fig. 2.7. Relationship between resilience, vulnerability and adaptive capacity.

2.6.1 *Resilience and vulnerability*

In the context of critical infrastructure systems, Haimes (2004) defined vulnerability to be the manifestations of the inherent states of the system that renders it susceptible to damage or loss. Sheffi (2005) characterizes the system's vulnerability as a combination of the likelihood of a disruption and the potential severity of the disruption. A system with low vulnerability has a low probability of disruption with light consequences, while a system has high vulnerability when the probability of a disruption is high and the consequences are severe. Figure 2.8 illustrates Sheffi's dimensions of vulnerability.

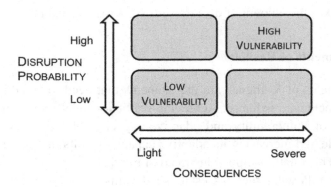

Fig. 2.8. Dimensions of vulnerability. Source: Sheffi (2005).

Dalziell and MacManus (2004) define a system of high vulnerability as a system that may be easily pushed from one state of stability or equilibrium to another, whereas it is not easy to push a system with low vulnerability from a state of stability or equilibrium.

Several studies establish the linkages between vulnerability and resilience. Gallopin (2006) relates resilience to the capacity of response, which he categorizes as a component of vulnerability. He also argues that even though a resilient system is less vulnerable, the relationship between the two is not symmetrical. Dalziell and MacManus (2004) refer to resilience as being a function of both the vulnerability of the system and its adaptive capacity. The relationship between resilience and vulnerability is bidirectional: loss of resilience will result in the increasing vulnerability of the system and would increase the risk of shifting the system into an undesirable state (Resilience-Alliance 2007).

2.6.2 *Resilience and adaptive capacity*

The adaptive capacity of a system can be viewed as the capacity to adapt and to reconfigure in the face of disruptions without losing functionality (Resilience-Alliance 2007). It can also be viewed as the ability of a system to adjust to changing internal demands and external circumstances (Carpenter and Brock 2008).

Folke *et al.* (2002) define the adaptive capacity of the system to be the ability to cope with novel situations. Systems with a high adaptive capacity are able to reconfigure themselves while preserving functionality in the face of disruptions. Walker *et al.* (2004) define the adaptive capacity as a component that can be used to manage resilience. Gallopin (2006) suggests that the adaptive capacity of the system is an attribute that exists before the occurrence of a disruption.

Dalziell and McManus (2004) refer to resilience as a function of adaptive capacity and vulnerability. The adaptive capacity quality of the system before a disruptive event is an indication of the likelihood of successful adaptation following a disruptive event. More resilient systems have a larger adaptive capacity envelope, which enables the system to cope with changes imposed by a disruptive event.

2.7 Resilience in Organizations

Infrastructure systems have several layers amongst which is the organizational layer. Therefore, no infrastructure resilience discussion is complete without addressing the organizational aspect of infrastructure systems.

Organizations and enterprises are human-intensive systems that do not have a physical network for operation. In this type of system, people are themselves the physical infrastructure. Organizational systems have both the merits and drawbacks of being human-intensive systems. During disruptive events, people can make adjustments to improve the situation; compensating, recovering and compromising. However, humans also make mistakes and even violations (Reason 2001).

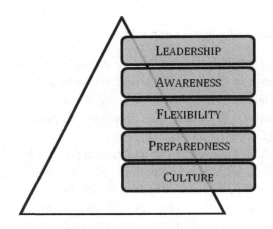

Fig. 2.9. Factors for achieving organizational resilience.

Figure 2.9 identifies several key factors that lead to a resilient organizational structure. These are elaborated upon in the following:

- **Leadership**

This is the most important element in organizational resilience. Enterprise leadership is about setting priorities, making commitments and the ability to make the right decisions about the courses of action to take when faced with adverse situations (O'Rourke 2007).

- **Awareness**

Resilient organizations monitor change that occurs within the organization and are hence able to identify disruptions in advance. Data gathering provides management with the current state of affairs and reveals the extent of the problem as well as how prepared the organization is to deal with it (Wreathall 2006). Good communication is key to raising awareness. An organization with a strong communications infrastructure can more easily detect disruptions and alert the responsible persons.

- **Preparedness/Emergency Planning**

Organizations can actively anticipate problems and prepare for them by building a team that is able to imagine different possibilities and is able to apply inventive solutions (Johnson-Lenz 2009). Frequently deployed and even necessary schemes in emergency planning are emergency drill-response exercises (O'Rourke 2007). These exercises prepare the organization to deal with problems by training individuals in the courses of action to take in the event of emergencies.

- **Flexibility**

Flexibility allows organizations to adapt to new problems. Resilience through flexibility is achieved by allowing individuals in the organization to make decisions (Wreathall 2006). Flexibility is also achieved by creating redundancy or backup systems. Cross-training within an organization allows individuals to substitute for one another to a certain extent in cases of emergency.

- **Culture**

Resilience is achieved through a culture that is built on trust and accountability (Bell 2002), engaging individuals at all levels by developing a sense of shared purpose (Johnson–Lenz 2009), encouraging a culture that is more aware of its environment, and supporting communication throughout the organization (Wreathall 2006).

In organizational theory, loose coupling is a conceptual tool that coordinates the interactions between actors and specifies a certain course of action. Grote (2006) suggests the application of loose coupling in organizations to enhance resilience. The following are four examples of loose coupling that are in line with the aforementioned factors for achieving resilience in organizations:

(i)   motivation through task orientation,

(ii) higher-order autonomy,

(iii) flexible changes between organizational modes, and

(iv) culture as basis for coordination/integration.

2.8 Resilience and Risk Management

Risk management deals with the identification of threats and vulnerabilities to determine risk and to apply mitigation strategies that reduce or avoid that risk. On the other hand, resilience is the ability of the system to cope with disruptive events so that the system can resume its regular functionality. Moody (2007), the president of the Critical Infrastructure Protection (CIP) program, related risk management and resilience in the following statement:

> Resilience is the empowerment of being aware of your situation, your risks, vulnerabilities and current capabilities to deal with them, and being able to make informed tactical and strategic decisions.

Risk management and resilience go hand in hand. Risk management procedures are used for the identification of schemes that enhance resilience based on the vulnerabilities of the system and their potential impact. Implementation of the schemes requires an evaluation of the available options in terms of cost-benefit tradeoffs and the implications of current decisions for the future.

Risk management applies measures such as detection and prevention that affect vulnerability while preserving the original inherent state of the system (Haimes 2006). Achieving resilience in systems extends beyond making the system less vulnerable to disruptions; it also entails the implementation of adaptive measures that will enable the system to resume functionality with minimum losses if a threat does impact the system.

In terms of critical infrastructures, Haimes (2006) states that the solution to infrastructure security is a result of protection and resilience. He refers to protection as the set of risk management activities that reduce the vulnerability of the system, whereas resilience includes risk management activities that enable the system to withstand major disruptions within acceptable cost and time limits.

2.9 Summary

This chapter began by defining resilience and asserting why resilience also applies to engineering systems. Resilience is a topic often discussed by stakeholders; the September 11 attacks in the U.S. are in large part responsible for the growing interest in building resilience into systems of all kinds. Although the primary focus of discussion is resilience in engineering and infrastructure systems, resilience finds its roots in ecological systems, in psychology and in materials science.

A review of the literature reveals several definitions of resilient systems. The qualities of a resilient system are illustrated in Fig. 2.10.

Fig. 2.10. Qualities of a resilient system.

A resilient system can:

- absorb and contain shock,
- reorganize after a disturbance to resume functionality,
- apply adaptive responses in the face of threats,
- cope with hazards, and
- recover quickly from a disruption.

Resilience is a mechanism by which the infrastructure system can prepare itself against disruptive events. The factors that can potentially cause disruptive events have been categorized into human, natural, organizational and technical factors.

Researchers have put forward several proposals for measuring infrastructure resilience, especially after seismic events. Also, several metrics have been suggested to measure the resilience of service infrastructure systems. However, no common framework for measuring resilience has emerged to date.

Resilience is achieved by addressing the two elements of resilience: vulnerability and adaptive capacity. A resilient response reduces the vulnerability of the system and increases its adaptive capacity. Reducing the vulnerability allows the system to absorb shock; increasing its adaptive capacity allows the system to reconfigure and continue functionality in adverse situations.

Infrastructure systems are socio-technical components where the organizational layer of the infrastructure plays a role that is as important as that of the physical layer. The key factors for achieving organizational resilience are leadership, awareness, flexibility and culture.

This chapter also presented an overview of the relationship between resilience and risk management.

Chapter 3

Relationship Between Reliability, Robustness, Flexibility, Agility and Resilience

The previous chapter gave a definition of resilience and outlined what resilience means for infrastructure systems. This chapter aims to distinguish between resilience and other known system properties— namely, reliability, robustness, flexibility and agility. These terms often appear together in the literature; the first three are often referred to as the 3R's (Larson *et al.* 2005). Flexibility is what helps the system to bounce back and it has been defined as one way of achieving resilience (Sheffi 2005). The term "agility" is often used interchangeably with flexibility. The various definitions of these terms and how they relate to one another can be rather confusing. In this chapter, we attempt to clarify the relationship between these terms.

In the systems engineering context, these properties, among others, are often referred to as "ilities," since many of them end with "ility." However, an increasing number of terms that do not share this common ending fall under this category, such as robustness. Although an "ility" is not a dictionary term, it is generally understood as a characteristic or quality of a system that defines how well a system does what it is supposed to do. The "ilities" are emergent properties of the system that describe the desired characteristics the system should exhibit once it is completed, and they are used as the current measure for "state-of-the-art" (Han 2006).

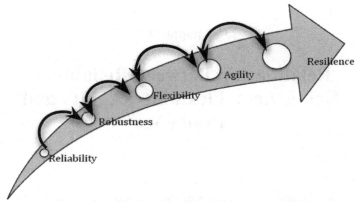

Fig. 3.1. Chapter outline.

Figure 3.1 shows the order in which these system properties are reviewed in this chapter. The relationships between each of these system properties, as well as their relationship to resilience, are indicated by the arrows in the figure. These system properties are then compared in terms of uncertainty, type of failure and adaptability.

These system properties — reliability, robustness, flexibility, agility and resilience — will be referred to as R^2FAR throughout the chapter.

3.1 Reliability

3.1.1 *Definition*

Reliability is defined as the ability of a system to function in a satisfactory manner in its predicted lifetime under stated conditions. From a mathematical perspective, reliability is a measure of the likelihood of failure-free performance over a specified period of time under stated conditions (DoD 1970). Reliable systems are dependable and steadfast. They are not prone to breakdown caused by component failure.

3.1.2 *Reliability metrics*

The most commonly used reliability metric is the reliability index, which is based on probabilistic data. The index has a value from 0 to 1, with 0 being the lowest reliability and 1 the highest.

A system's reliability is also characterized by the Mean Time to Failure (MTTF) and the Mean Time to Repair (MTTR). Systems with higher MTTF and MTTR values are more reliable (Marshall and Chapman 2002).

MTTF is applied to non-repairable physical components such as light bulbs. It is calculated from data taken over a period of time:

$$\text{MTTF} = \frac{\text{Total operating time for all components}}{\text{No. of failures over that time}} . \tag{3.1}$$

MTTR is a measure of the average time that a piece of equipment performs its function without requiring repair. As MTTF and MTTR are statistical quantities, a large number of failures must be recorded to have confidence in the results.

The computational techniques used for optimizing the reliability of systems include reliability block diagrams, where the system is represented as a series-parallel network. Series-parallel systems consist of a number of parallel subsystems that are connected in series. The components are characterized by their reliability and cost. Equation (3.2) shows the formula used for calculating the reliability of a series-parallel system.

$$R = \prod_{i=1}^{s}\left(1 - \prod_{j=1}^{n_i}(1 - r_{ij})^{x_{ij}}\right), \tag{3.2}$$

where s is the number of subsystems, i is the index for the subsystems, n is the total number of components used in a pure parallel system, x_{ij} is the quantity of component j used in subsystem i, r_{ij} is the reliability of component j in subsystem i, and c_{ij} is the cost of component j in subsystem i.

Fault tree analysis, another way of representing reliability block diagrams, uses logic gates to connect the system components. Reliability graphs represent the system as a network. Linear transformations such as genetic algorithms and probabilistic seismic demand analysis (PSDA) are also used for measuring a system's reliability.

3.1.3 *Reliability and resilience*

Critical infrastructure systems are crucial for everyday activities and hence reliability is a requirement of these systems. The National Infrastructure Protection Plan (NIPP) lists both reliability and resilience as measures to mitigate vulnerabilities in order to protect critical infrastructure systems and stresses the reliability of energy grid systems (NIPP 2009). The Department of Energy (DOE) has several programs that increase the reliability and resilience of the U.S. energy infrastructure: addressing energy storage issues, grid interconnection and usage of renewable energy sources (Anderson 2001).

The traditional reliability criteria ensure that a system operates without failure under known circumstances, such as a sudden but expected increase in demand, which is an eventuality that commonly occurs in power networks. However, unforeseen disruptive events compromise a system's reliability. Truly reliable systems should function in the expected manner even after the occurrence of unforeseen disruptive events. Therefore, it is important to make these systems resilient as well as reliable.

The differences between reliability and resilience can be summarized as follows:

Reliability	**Resilience**
• Designed for known failure circumstances	• Designed for unforeseen disruptive events
• Failures are internal	• Failures are external
• System cannot reconfigure to avoid failure	• System can reconfigure to continue operation

Figure 3.2 shows the Venn diagram of the reliability and resilience.

RELIABILITY	RESILIENCE
Known failure circumstances	Unknown failure circumstances
Internal disruptions	Severe external failures
No adaptability	Adaptability

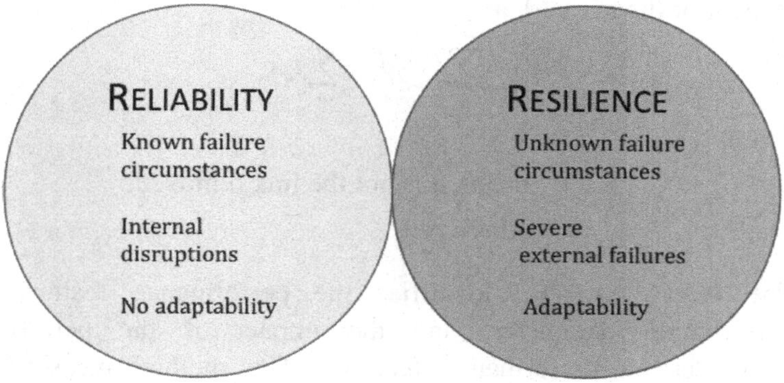

Fig. 3.2. Venn diagram of reliability and resilience.

3.2 Robustness

3.2.1 *Definition*

Robustness has been defined as a property that the system exhibits across a wide range of operational conditions (Gribble 2001). Moses (2004) defines a robust system as one that is able to maintain its original functionality as much as possible when changes are made to it.

Another definition of robustness in social and ecological systems is the capacity of the system to maintain performance when subjected to internal and external unpredictable perturbations (Janssen 2007). The same definition may be applied to engineering systems in general as well as infrastructure systems in particular.

3.2.2 *Robustness metrics*

As with resilience, researchers are still investigating ways to quantify robustness. Several approaches have been introduced to measure robustness, including:

- The Network Robustness Index (NRI); identifies the critical links in, and evaluates the network performance of, networked infrastructure systems — in particular the transportation infrastructure (Scott *et al.* 2005). The NRI calculates the importance of a link a with network flow x_a and traveled time t_a compared to the rest of the network as:

$$\text{NRI} = \sum_a t_a x_a \delta_a - \sum_a t_a x_a \,, \qquad (3.3)$$

where

$$\delta_a = \begin{cases} 1 & \text{if link } a \text{ is not the link removed,} \\ 0 & \text{otherwise.} \end{cases}$$

- The FePIA process; identifies the performance features, the perturbation parameter, and the impact of the perturbation parameter on performance features. The method measures the Probabilistic Robustness Index (PRI) in terms of direct and indirect risk (Baker *et al.* 2008). The index is derived from direct and indirect risk, and is measured as:

$$\text{I}_{\text{Rob}} = \frac{\text{Direct Risk} + \text{Indirect Risk}}{\text{Direct Risk}} \,. \qquad (3.4)$$

- The Dynamic Network Robustness (DYNER) method; measures the robustness of networks to node deletion while considering backup systems (Singer 2006).

3.2.3 *Robustness and reliability*

The main difference between robustness and reliability lies in the sources of disruptions (Whitson and Ramirez–Marquez 2009). In reliability, the sources of disruptions are internal, whereas in robustness they are internal as well as external (Janssen 2007). Reliability is defined in terms of lifetime. This definition applies to physical components that make up a physical system. The lifetime of infrastructure systems is as long as the system is usable/needed.

3.2.4 *Robustness and resilience*

Robust systems are able to continue operation in their original form (Hudsal 2008); that is, the structure of the system does not adapt to the disruptions but withstands them. Robustness does not specify the course of action or the behavior of the system undergoing a disruptive event; it is the resilient behavior that the system exhibits that allows it to adapt or reconfigure in the face of disruptions such that it can resume normal operations.

Considering natural disasters, Bruneau *et al.* (2003) define robustness as the ability of the system to withstand the damage induced by disasters without significant degradation in performance. In this context, these authors identify robustness as one of the properties of resilience; that is, making the systems more robust is one step towards resilience.

The similarities and differences between robustness and resilience are as follows:

Robustness	**Resilience**
• Designed for known uncertainties	• Designed for known and unknown uncertainties
• Failures are internal and external	• Severe internal and external failures
• Maintains functionality in the same form	• Adapts to changing circumstances

The Venn diagram shown in Fig. 3.3 illustrates the similarities and differences between robustness and resilience.

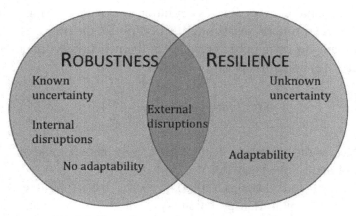

Fig. 3.3. Venn diagram of robustness and resilience.

3.3 Flexibility

3.3.1 *Definition*

In engineering systems, the general essence of flexibility is that it is the ability of the system to adapt to its environment due to unforeseen but expected circumstances. It has also been defined as the ability of the system to respond to potential internal or external changes affecting its value delivery in a timely and cost-effective manner (Nilchiani 2005). Moses (2004) defines a flexible system by the ease with which changes may be made to it; Nilchiani (2005) extends this view to networked systems, where she considers the ease of adding new nodes to the network or introducing new paths for connecting nodes.

Flexibility in organizations has been defined by Westrum (2006) as the ability of an organization to reorganize itself in order to overcome problems.

3.3.2 *Flexibility metrics*

An extensive amount of research has been dedicated to the issue of flexibility in manufacturing systems. As this thesis focuses on networked infrastructure systems, the flexibility metrics reviewed in the following are those that address networked systems and networked infrastructure systems.

On a similar note to Moses's definition of flexibility, Magee and De Weck (2002) propose measuring flexibility as the ratio of distinct network paths to the number of nodes in the network. Nilchiani (2005) formulates this relationship as:

$$Flexibility\_measure = \frac{N_{paths}}{n_{nodes}}, \qquad (3.5)$$

where N_{paths} is the number of distinct paths in the network and n_{nodes} is the number of nodes in the network.

Nilchiani and Hastings (2003) proposes measuring the network flexibility of orbital transportation systems using a combination of several metrics: *mix flexibility*, for offering different types of services (long-term); *volume flexibility*, for coping with different demands (mid-term); and *emergency service flexibility*, for providing unscheduled emergency services (short-term). The three types of flexibility are measured as shown in Eqs. (3.6)–(3.8).

- Mix flexibility, f_m:

$$f_m = \frac{S_m - E_m}{S - E},$$ (3.6)

where E is the total system cost over the system's lifetime, S is the total revenue over the system's lifetime, and m denotes the type of service.

- Volume flexibility, f_v:

$$f_v = \frac{\int_0^E e^{-rt_m}(S - E)p(S)dS}{NPV},$$ (3.7)

where t_m is the time period after which the system operates with a mature client base, E is the total system cost over the system's lifetime, S is the total revenue over the system's lifetime, NPV is the risk-free investment return, and $p(S)$ is the log-normal distribution of system revenues.

- Emergency service flexibility, f_e:

$$f_e = \frac{Cap_{max}}{Cap_{current}},$$ (3.8)

where Cap_{max} and $Cap_{current}$ are the maximum and current service capacity of the system.

Considering transportation infrastructure systems, Morlok and Chang (2004) measure the flexibility of transportation networks as the maximum demand that the network can accommodate when subjected to fixed Origin-Destination traffic patterns and deviations from it. They propose the use of the MAXCAP and ADDVOL optimization models for measuring the maximum demand. The MAXCAP model is based on fixed Origin-Destination traffic patterns whereas ADDVOL allows for the deviation from the base traffic pattern.

3.3.3 *Flexibility and robustness*

Moses (2004) distinguishes between flexibility and robustness in terms of the system's goal. While the main goal of flexibility is to add or modify the functions, the goal of a robust system is to maintain the original function as much as possible. Therefore, a flexible system is likely to be robust if the system can easily accommodate the changes that will make it more robust (Nilchiani 2005).

3.3.4 *Flexibility and resilience*

Flexibility allows the system to adapt to new circumstances. Adaptation is also a feature of resilient systems. Sheffi (2005) sees flexibility as a way of building resilience into systems, as it allows systems to respond quickly to disruptions. Flexibility has also been identified as one of the attributes of resilient systems because it allows systems to adapt and restructure in the face of disruptions (Jackson 2009).

Both flexibility and resilience entail having a higher tolerance to external forces and disruptions. A flexible object can break when sufficient force is applied to it while a resilient system is able to endure severe disruptions and it will not break under the application of force but will continue to function.

Flexibility allows systems to cope with gradual or abrupt changes. On the other hand, resilience is mainly implemented in systems to help the system cope with abrupt changes.

Another feature that distinguishes flexibility from resilience is the functionality of the system. Whereas flexibility allows the system to be used for other functions than the one it was originally designed for, resilience allows the system to continue to deliver the same value delivery when dealing with new situations.

The above points can be summarized as follows:

Flexibility	**Resilience**
• Adapts easily to unforeseen circumstances	• Able to adapt to unforeseen circumstances
• Failures are internal and external	• Severe internal and external failures
• High tolerance to failure	• High tolerance to failure
• Can be fragile	• Not fragile
• Designed for abrupt and gradual changes	• Designed to cope with abrupt changes
• May be used to deliver different functionality	• Used for the same purpose

Figure 3.4. shows the Venn representation of the above-mentioned points.

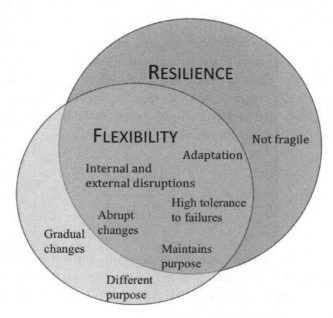

Fig. 3.4. Venn diagram of flexibility and resilience.

3.4 Agility

3.4.1 *Definition*

The concept of agility has been growing with increasing momentum in the last couple of decades. The general consensus is that agility is the ability of the system to adapt rapidly to new situations (Schulz and Fricke 1999). It has also been described as the ability to apply new ideas and to be creative in the face of adverse situations (Boehm and Turner 2004). Agile systems are readily reconfigured to incorporate significant new design features in a shorter period of time and in a more assured manner (Amin and Horowitz 2008).

3.4.2 *Agility metrics*

Researchers have put forward several methods for measuring agility in different disciplines, such as manufacturing systems (Sieger *et al.* 2000), supply chain management (Bottani 2006), and enterprise systems. Some of the metrics proposed for measuring enterprise systems are as follows:

- The Agility Index (AI) is a weighted sum of an agility matrix that defines the strategic value of an enterprise in terms of its time performance (Kumar and Motwani 1995). The matrix cells represent all combinations of time to market segments (e.g., development and production) and agility determinants (e.g., time). The Agility Index is measured as:

$$\text{AI} = \frac{\sum_{I=1}^{I=sj} \sum_{j=1}^{j=F} \sum_{k=1}^{k=fj} \left\{ W_i U_{jk} Y_{ij} \right\}}{\sum_{I=1}^{I=s} \sum_{j=1}^{j=F} \sum_{k=1}^{k=F} 10 \left\{ W_i U_{jk} \right\}} , \qquad (3.9)$$

where i is the segment index, j is the agility influencing factor, jk is the index of sub-factors, F is the number of sub-factors, W_i is the agility weight assignment, U_{jk} is the agility weight, and Y_{ij} is the agility-weight earned by a firm for cell ij.

- The Total Agility Index (TAI) measures network agility using a mathematical function obtained by the summation of weighted agility drivers of the network constituents such as time, cost or quality (Mansouri *et al.* 2009a). The Total Agility Index is formulated as:

$$TAI = \sum_{i=1}^{N} w_i a_i^2 , \tag{3.10}$$

where a_i is the agility factor for the ith constituent system and w_i is the associated weight.

- Ganguly *et al.* (2009) propose measuring enterprise agility as a vector of market share AG(Ms), responsiveness AG(Re) and cost effectiveness AG(Ce). These metrics measure quality, speed and cost, respectively. The three agility metrics are formulated as:

$$AG(Ms) = \frac{\text{Market share of an enterprise } (p = n)}{\text{Market share of an enterprise } (p = 1)} , \tag{3.11}$$

$$AG(Re) = \frac{\text{Avg NPD cycle for industry}}{\text{Avg NPD cycle for measured enterprise}} , \tag{3.12}$$

$$AG(Ce) = \frac{\text{Avg cost NPD cycle for industry}}{\text{Avg cost of NPD cycle for measured enterprise}} , \tag{3.13}$$

where p is the market cycle for a comparable and substitutable product family produced for the market, or the average product development cycle for that particular market, and NPD denotes new product development.

3.4.3 *Agility and flexibility*

The terms "agility" and "flexibility" are interchangeably used in the literature. This is because they both deal with the ability of systems to adapt to new circumstances. However, agility is not only the ability to adapt to new circumstances; it is the ease with which the system adapts.

For example, to be a good dancer, one must have a high degree of flexibility; the body must be able to twist and turn into unusual positions. But it is the fluidity of movement that makes a great dancer. Thus, more agile systems exhibit a higher or better level of adaptation.

3.4.4 *Agility and resilience*

Both resilience and agility deal with adaptation in the face of adverse situations. In order to distinguish between these two terms, it is important to review the definition of resilience. Resilience is made up of two components: first, that the system can absorb shock; second, that it is able to adapt to change. Both agility and flexibility allow the system to adapt to new situations. However, a resilient system is also, as much as possible, able to absorb shock caused by severe disruptions.

The similarities and differences between agility and resilience are summarized as follows:

Agility	**Resilience**
• Able to adapt to new situations	• Adapts following a disruptive event
• Exhibits rapid adaptation	• Recovers quickly from disruptions
• Benefits from new situations	• Maintains system's value delivery
• Failures are internal and external	• Severe internal and external failures

The Venn diagram in Fig. 3.5 illustrates these similarities and differences.

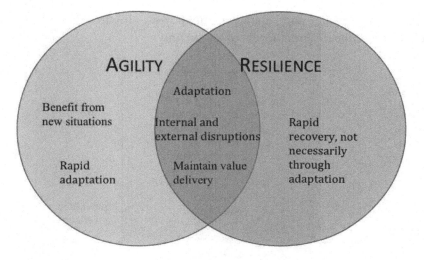

Fig. 3.5. Venn diagram of agility and resilience.

3.5 Comparing R²FAR in Terms of Type Failures, Uncertainty and Adaptability

In the previous sections, the components of R^2FAR were compared to one another and to resilience. The comparison showed that the main similarities and differences are in what the system is prepared for (type of failure), what causes those failures (uncertainty), and how the system reacts to overcome the failure (level of adaptability).

The types of failure are either internal or external. Internal failures are due to failures in the system components while external failures are triggered by the environment. A reliable system is characterized by its response to internal failures. Meanwhile, robustness, flexibility and agility are characterized by the system's response to both internal and external failures. Resilience is the ability of the system to overcome severe internal and external disruptions.

There are several categories for the uncertainties that cause disruptions in systems. According to Hastings and McManus (2004), uncertainties have different levels. They may arise due to lack of knowledge, lack of definition, statistically characterized phenomena, known unknowns, and unknown unknowns. Figure 3.6 shows a schematic of the different levels of uncertainty.

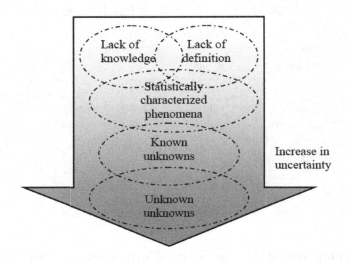

Fig. 3.6. Schematic of the depth and level of uncertainty in a system. Source: Nilchiani (2005).

The R^2FAR discussion is based on disruptions that impede the performance of systems that were otherwise fully functional, thus excluding lack of knowledge, lack of definition and statistical characterization uncertainties. Failures due to known unknowns are based on the probability that a disruption might occur. Unknown unknowns are unexpected and unforeseen.

Disruptions such as natural disasters or technological failures may be categorized as known unknowns since it may be possible to foresee the occurrence of these events, but a terrorist attack is an unknown unknown uncertainty. Increasing the reliability of the system through the use of better, higher quality components and redundancy allocation optimization techniques reduces the susceptibility of the system to known unknowns. Robustness, flexibility and agility are measures taken against unknown unknown uncertainty. Implementing resilience in systems prepares them in the face of known unknowns such as natural disasters as well as unknown unknowns such as terrorist attacks.

The third and final difference between the components in R^2FAR is the reaction of the system to overcoming failures. Considering reliability and robustness, the basic structure of the system remains unchanged; the system does not adapt to the disruption but tries to overcome it in its current structure. Considering flexibility, agility and resilience, the system adapts to the disruptions through reconfiguration. Figure 3.7 summarizes the points mentioned above.

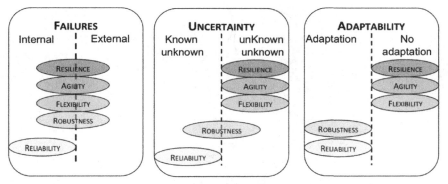

Fig. 3.7. Similarities and differences between the components of R^2FAR.

3.6 Summary

This chapter included a synopsis of reliability, robustness, flexibility and agility consisting of definitions and metrics, and the similarities and differences between them. These system properties were discussed in terms of their relationship to one another as well as to resilience.

Reliability is the ability of the system to withstand internal disruptions. Robustness is the ability of the system to endure external and internal disruptions without adapting. Flexibility allows the system to adapt to new circumstances easily. Agility is the speed by which the system can adapt to new situations as well as benefit from the change. Resilience is the ability of the system to withstand and endure severe disruptions, and to be able to maintain functionality through adaptation if necessary. These system properties differ from each other with respect to the types of failures, causes of failures, and the reaction of the system to failures.

In summary, we can conclude that while reliability is a basic requirement of the system, robustness, flexibility and agility are all measures that can be taken to achieve resilience in infrastructure systems. This relationship is illustrated in Fig. 3.8.

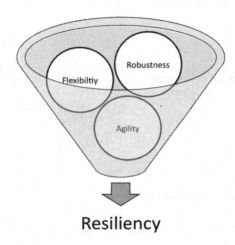

Fig. 3.8. Relationship between robustness, flexibility, agility and resilience.

Chapter 4

Resilience-Enabling Schemes

Resilience-enabling schemes are the design principles that are used to prepare infrastructure systems against unexpected system shocks. System shocks such as natural disasters are unavoidable, and in some cases, the time of occurrence and magnitude of change is unpredictable. The question is how to enable the infrastructures to withstand and survive these hazards and the major changes associated with them, with minimum or no loss.

The answer lies in making infrastructure systems more resilient in the face of major threats and hazards. This statement raises a further question: What measures can be taken to achieve resilience? To answer this question, we refer to the definition of resilience and the elements that constitute a resilient system. We define resilience as the ability of the system to be less susceptible to disruptions as well as to be able to recover rapidly from a disruption such that the system can return to, or closely approach, its original service delivery levels.

As mentioned in Chap. 2, Dalizell and McManus (2004) suggested that resilience is made up of two elements: vulnerability and adaptive capacity. Resilience in systems is achievable by reducing the system's vulnerability and increasing its adaptive capacity. Less vulnerable systems are less susceptible to disruptions. The adaptive capacity component of resilience allows the system to continue to function and deliver the expected value delivery levels through reconfiguration in the face of disruptions (Resilience-Alliance 2007). If necessary, the system undergoes changes of its basic structure in order to continue operation.

Figure 4.1 shows the two elements for achieving resilience in infrastructure systems.

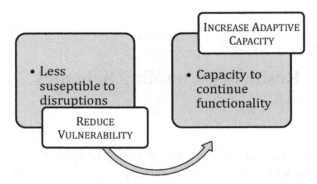

Fig. 4.1. The two elements for achieving resilience.

Resilience-enabling schemes are the measures taken to implement or increase resilience in systems. They are either proactive or reactive. Vulnerability reduction is a proactive scheme that mitigates the consequences of disruptive events by applying preventive measures before their occurrence. Reducing the vulnerability reduces the probability of potential losses, thereby minimizing the magnitude of damage (Uribe *et al.* 1999). The adaptive capacity component enables the system to recover after the occurrence of the disruptive event; hence, it is a reactive measure.

This chapter proposes several schemes that aid in achieving resilience in infrastructure systems. These resilience-enabling schemes have been taken from the literature through the identification of the various methods that have been suggested to improve the quality of service of systems undergoing disruptive events.

4.1 Scheme Identification

In this chapter, resilience-enabling schemes are categorized into those that reduce the vulnerability and those that increase the adaptive capacity of systems. The vulnerability reduction schemes include redundancy, diversity, hardening, capacity tolerance, and modularity. The schemes that increase adaptive capacity are resource allocation, preparedness, collaboration, and cognition.

Choosing the appropriate resilience scheme(s) depends on the type of infrastructure system and the focus of its stakeholders. In some cases, the objective may be to reduce the infrastructure system's vulnerability, if the adaptive capacity component of the system is seen as sufficient by stakeholders, or *vice versa*. The categorization of resilience enablers is shown in Fig. 4.2.

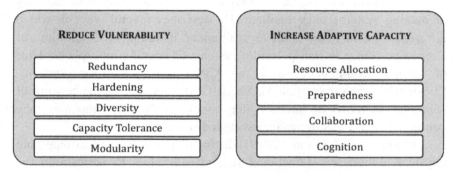

Fig. 4.2. Resilience enablers for vulnerability reduction and increasing adaptive capacity.

4.2 Vulnerability Reduction

Threats and hazards such as malicious attacks and natural disasters, if severe enough, can degrade the quality of operation of vulnerable infrastructure systems. The vulnerability reduction component of achieving resilience in systems aims at preparing the system in the face of disruptions. Reducing vulnerability makes the system less susceptible to disruptions and hence minimizes potential damage or loss. This chapter identifies the following schemes that enable infrastructure systems to be less vulnerable: redundancy, hardening, diversity, capacity tolerance, and modularity. The following sections will elaborate on each of these resilience schemes.

4.2.1 *Redundancy*

In physical infrastructure systems, redundancy refers to the existence of parallel systems that can assume operation when the original system fails. Generally speaking, redundant elements offer a lower quality of service than the main system. However, service degradation is gradual, and losses are minimized until the full operational capacity of the main system is restored.

Bruneau *et al.* (2003) have identified redundancy as one of the dimensions of resilience. Redundancy refers to the extent to which elements, systems and other measures of analysis are substitutable in the event of a disruption. Haimes (2006) identifies redundancy to be one way of making systems more resilient. He describes several ways in which different systems can achieve resilience, including the addition of alternative routes in transportation systems or creating multiple backups of critical components such as CPUs in information systems. Considering enterprise systems, Sheffi (2005) formulates the concept of resilience in terms of having safety stocks such that companies may continue to serve customers following a disruption.

Madni and Jackson (2009) distinguish between functional and physical redundancy. Functional redundancy refers to performing the same task using a different system whereas physical redundancy is through the repetition of elements in the system. These two types of redundancy exist in infrastructure systems such as the Internet telecommunication systems, where undersea cables provide the communication channels between continents. Figure 4.3 shows the redundancy in the global Internet communication infrastructure system in the cables connecting South-East Asia to West Europe, where SEA-ME-WE-4 is used as a redundant cable in the case of repairs or operational failures within SEA-ME-WE-3.

One disadvantage of physical redundancy is that it is often not possible to build a fully redundant system due to the high overheads associated with building and maintaining such systems (Haimes *et al.* 2008).

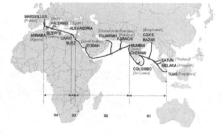

(i) SEA-ME-WE3	(ii) SEA-ME-WE4
Source: *www.smw3.com*	Source: *www.seamewe4.com*

Fig. 4.3. Physical redundancy in SEA-ME-WE3 and SEA-ME-WE4 cable systems.

Functional redundancy is in the form of parallel systems such as free space optical systems or satellites. It is referred to as Diversity in the following section since it entails the existence of parallel systems deployable during disruptive events.

4.2.2 *Diversity*

As the saying goes, "Don't put all your eggs in one basket"; diversification of people and resources is a step towards achieving resilience (Goble *et al.* 2002). Diversity in infrastructure systems is achievable by having loosely coupled services that can be joined together or disassembled to meet demand in order to support the functionality of the infrastructure. The alternative system should be able to provide the same quality of service as the primary system in the case of a disruption.

In communications infrastructure systems, there may be multiple modes of transferring data, such as via copper wires or optical fiber cables, free-space optical communication or even via satellite (PSHSB 2008). In the energy infrastructure systems, having the option of using alternate renewable energy resources rather than depending primarily on fossil fuels is a form of diversity. At the electricity generation level, it is the ability of a power plant to switch from oil to coal if the oil supply is disrupted, or *vice versa* (Pommerening 2007). Diverse sources of renewable energy generation are shown in Fig. 4.4.

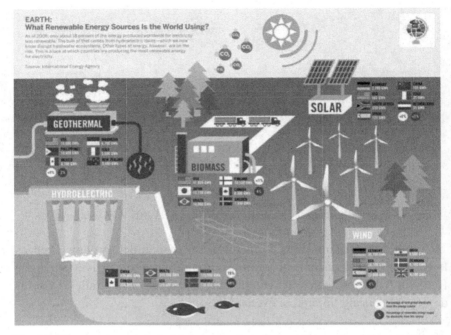

Fig. 4.4. Diverse sources of electricity generation. Source: International Energy Agency
http://www.iea.org/

4.2.3 *Hardening*

Hardening refers to the fortification of the infrastructure system in order
to promote structural integrity (Goble *et al.* 2002). In this scheme,
infrastructure is prevented from easily succumbing to threats by using
better quality system components (Jackson 2009; Perelman 2007;
Pommerening 2007). Hardening minimizes the potential damage caused
by disruptions, which will in turn reduce recovery efforts and the time it
takes for the infrastructure system to resume operation. The National
Infrastructure Protection Plan (NIPP 2009) promotes the hardening of
key resources as a way of protecting these critical assets and ensuring
resilience.

This scheme is often deployed in the electrical grid system, where
hardening efforts focus on the use of better poles and lines that can
withstand extreme weather conditions or using underground power lines

(Kema 2010). For the Internet, it has been suggested to use "hardened routers," where some of the functions of the routers are enhanced through cryptography. Here, hardening is a security measure for enhancing the resilience of the Internet to attacks instead of the traditional firewalls and filtering programs (Zhang and Dasgupta 2003).

In the transportation infrastructure, hardening has also been set as a core goal for improving the security of air and ground transportation systems, which include the waterways and ports of the maritime infrastructure. Hardening of the maritime infrastructure may be in the form of deployment of CCTV, better lighting and fencing, and thorough container inspection (GOHS 2010).

4.2.4 *Capacity tolerance*

A system that operates within its demand limits is prone to operational failure due to slight disruptions. The Capacity Tolerance scheme implies that the localized capacity of the system should be able to operate beyond these regular demand limits (Jackson 2009). As Fig. 4.5 shows, in addition to the normal demand margin, systems designed with an additional shock absorption margin do not easily succumb to disruptions. Implementing this is a challenging task, however, since the defined margins may erode over time due to increasing demand (Woods 2005).

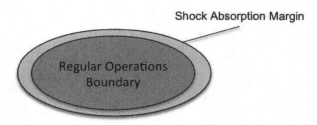

Fig. 4.5. The challenge of defining system boundaries. Adapted from Jackson (2009).

In the transportation infrastructure, it may be undesirable to design roads that meet a much higher demand than predicted, since more people would be encouraged to use cars instead of public transportation. However, traffic congestion has negative economic, environmental and psychological impacts. Setting boundaries that span regular operations, the margin for shock absorption and the safety envelope is a challenging task; the road infrastructure network brings up the question of quality versus quantity.

The Capacity Tolerance scheme is often deployed for rerouting flow over network links that have residual capacities. Depending on the type of infrastructure system, the flow may be mass, data, energy, etc. In the telecommunication network, rerouting of data packets using the network's residual capacity effectively improves the system's resilience (Omer *et al.* 2009).

4.2.5 *Modularity*

Modular systems are those that can be easily separated and recombined. Since disruptive events may impact only certain parts of the system, modularity reduces the susceptibility of the system by making it easier to isolate the faulty part for repair or replacement.

Modularity reduces the system's complexity by reducing the number of interfaces (Thorogood and Yetton 2005). Additionally, a modular design creates systems that are scalable, changeable, swappable, and in some cases, portable (Niles 2005). Figure 4.6 is an illustration of non-modular versus modular design. Non-modular design entails using unique components and interfaces that are neither interchangeable nor swappable. Modular design is easier to understand, build and scale.

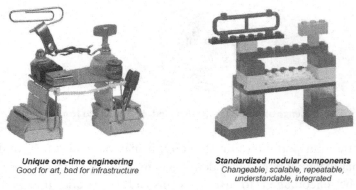

Unique one-time engineering
Good for art, bad for infrastructure

Standardized modular components
Changeable, scalable, repeatable,
understandable, integrated

Fig. 4.6. Non-modular versus modular design. Source: Niles (2005).

Modularity is also seen in the rail transportation infrastructure, where carriages are added or removed to change the size of the train. The same principle is used in the maritime infrastructure system, where containers all over the world are either 20 feet long or 40 feet long. (The most commonly used container size is the Twenty-foot Equivalent Unit, or TEU; *worldclassshipping.com*.)

Modularity is not limited to the physical components of the system. In organizations, modularity refers to the compartmentalization of the organizational structure (Calabretta 2009) and the automation of rules that govern the enterprise (Hutchinson 2006).

With respect to the human aspect, modularity makes things more understandable. Errors are avoided, problems are more readily anticipated, and information is more easily shared. All of these benefits lead to increased productivity (Niles 2005).

4.3 Increasing Adaptive Capacity Through Reorganization

Severe disruptions may render systems completely incapable of resuming functionality. The adaptive capacity component of resilience aims at ensuring continuation of service operation through reorganization. Systems with high adaptive capacity are able to reconfigure or reorganize their basic structure without a significant loss in functionality (Folke *et al.* 2002). The following sections elaborate on several schemes that enable the system to reorganize in order to increase adaptive capacity.

4.3.1 *Resource allocation*

Resource allocation refers to the manner in which resources are distributed in order to recover from disruptive events. Effective resource allocation requires the use of resources such as the physical capacity of the network, the equipment that facilitates the rerouting or redirection of the network flow and personnel in a timely manner. It also requires an accurate processing of the kind and quantity of resources needed so that the expected value delivery level of the infrastructure system is maintained.

Several studies have focused on the issue of resource allocation during emergencies — in particular for earthquake response. Researchers have developed optimization techniques that calculate the optimum resource allocation required by a region based on the severity of the disruptions and the available resources in its surroundings.

The National Infrastructure Protection Plan (NIPP 2009) stresses the importance of resource allocation in improving the resilience of critical infrastructure and key resources:

> Resources must be directed to the areas of greatest priority to enable effective management of risk. By definition, all CIKR[1] assets, systems, and networks are important.

A critical factor for the Resource Allocation scheme is the collaboration of the different entities and stakeholders involved in the relief efforts — the importance of which is discussed in the following section.

4.3.2 *Collaboration — United we stand*

Infrastructure systems do not, and cannot, exist independently. An infrastructure system consists of several subsystems that interact with one another as well as with other parallel infrastructure systems.

An individual networked infrastructure system can be thought of as a system of systems where the subsystems are interconnected (Jackson 2009). Collaborative capacity allows for seamless sharing, sending and receiving of information across all the subnetworks of the infrastructure system (Brown 2009).

A disruption rarely limits itself to one portion of the infrastructure system of systems; cascading failures propagate through the subsystems and may affect the whole network. A power failure in the electrical grid will impact the communications infrastructure, which relies primarily on powered technology. The impact of the power failure will also be felt in the transportation infrastructure, which relies on both the communication and the power infrastructures for its operation.

---

[1]CIKR: Critical Infrastructure and Key Resources

Within the organizational infrastructure, collaboration between different organizations promotes decentralization. Also, the fluid exchange of information promoted by collaborative efforts increases the resilience of infrastructure systems.

A well-known example is Hurricane Katarina, where centralized bureaucracy and the lack of communication between government agencies contributed to the adverse impact on New Orleans (Westrum 2006). Both of these factors are attributed to a lack of collaboration.

4.3.3 *Preparedness*

Planning ahead is a key factor in overcoming disruptions. The Preparedness scheme extends to the sociological aspect of infrastructure systems. Preparedness plans consist of policies that manage the consequences of threats and facilitate recovery procedures (Haimes *et al.* 2008).

Proper planning and preparedness has been proven to minimize the consequences of earthquakes. Both San Francisco and Armenia experienced earthquakes of magnitude 6.0–7.0 in 1988 and 1989, respectively. The losses suffered by San Francisco were 67 lives and US$7 billion in property. On the other hand, the death toll in Armenia was over 25,000 with the financial loss exceeded US$20 billion. While San Francisco recovered quickly, the impact of the devastating earthquake in Armenia is still felt today to some extent. Analysts believe that this was primarily due to the fact that San Francisco was prepared and Armenia was not (Besemer 2010).

In the face of overcoming disasters at the national level, the Department of Homeland Security issued the Homeland Security Presidential Directive (HSPD)-8. The directive focuses on ensuring the optimal level of preparedness to protect, prevent, respond to, and recover from the full range of natural and manmade hazards and threats (NIPP 2009).

4.3.4 *Cognition*

The final resilience-enabling scheme discussed in this section is Cognition. This scheme is a process that a system goes through rather than a single course of action or a predefined set of rules. Cognition is a broad topic that deals with many aspects of infrastructure systems including the organizational structure as well the physical and technical capabilities of the infrastructure. The following outlines the concept without going into detail.

The concept of cognition is closely related to drift correction (Leveson *et al.* 2006). Drift correction implies monitoring the system when it enters a region of risk and applying the appropriate responses. In cognition, the system is monitored continuously at all times. A cognitive system is able to perceive the changes that occur in it, select a course of action to deal with the current situation, and keep track of the system behavior for the implemented course of action for future reference.

A prerequisite of the cognitive process is the intelligence element, which is the component that enables the system to react in a cognitive manner. The cognitive process shown in Fig. 4.7 is a general framework that applies to both physical and organizational infrastructure systems.

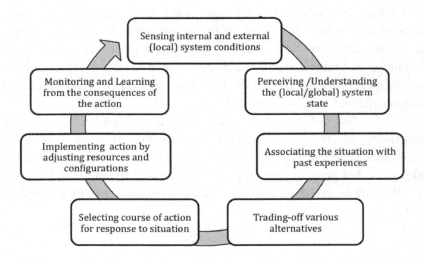

Fig. 4.7. Capabilities of cognition-centric systems. Source: Mostahari (2009).

Cognition in infrastructure systems not only creates resilient systems through the application of appropriate courses of action, but also optimizes the functionality of the infrastructure in order to better service those it was intended for in the first place — the people. In the transportation infrastructure, a cognitive system applies intelligent solutions to users based on the current and predicted states of the system. It continuously informs users about which roads to take or avoid, and which means of public transportation is the most convenient in terms of time, cost, etc. In the transportation infrastructure, instead of a simple rerouting of traffic (in the case of an accident) based on the current state of the system, cognition enables the system to predict the human response in the system based on previous incidents.

In order to execute cognitive behavior, a system requires many of the schemes described above, such as Redundancy, Modularity, Preparedness, Diversity, and Collaboration.

4.4 Summary

Building resilience into infrastructure systems is achievable through the implementation of schemes that enable the system to absorb the shock and maintain functionality when disruptions occur. This chapter reviewed several resilience-enabling schemes that fall into the categories of "vulnerability reduction" (reduction of susceptibility to disruptions) and "increased adaptive capacity" (reorganization to maintain functionality). This categorization is based on the elements of a resilient system discussed in Chap. 2.

The vulnerability reduction enabling schemes include redundancy, hardening, diversity, capacity tolerance, and modularity. Increased adaptive capacity is achievable through Resource Allocation, Collaboration, Preparedness, and Cognition. Some of these schemes relate to the infrastructure system's physical structure, while others relate to the organizational aspects of the infrastructure system, or both the social and technical aspects.

Chapter 5

Measuring the Resilience of Networked Infrastructure Systems

Implementing resilience in systems enables them to "bounce back" after the occurrence of disruptions. Although there is a strong emphasis on disruptions that are a result of malicious terrorist attacks, these types of disruptions are only a small fraction of those that typically assault infrastructure systems. It is crucial, for socioeconomic continuity, to consider all types of threats and hazards, natural or man-made, when building resilience into infrastructure systems. However, one cannot begin to implement resilience without knowledge of the following:

* the infrastructure system's current state of resilience,
* the benefits associated with implementing specific options for achieving/improving the infrastructure system's resilience.
* the acceptable level of resilience that needs to be incorporated,
* the available options for enhancing the resilience of the infrastructure system, and

This chapter begins with the risk analysis/identification process that gives stakeholders a better understanding of the threats and vulnerabilities of their respective infrastructure systems. Next, the Networked Infrastructure Resilience Assessment (NIRA) framework, which addresses the above-mentioned points, is presented. The general structure of the framework consists of a series of steps that can be applied to all types of networked infrastructure systems. The final section of this chapter links the NIRA framework to the field of systems engineering.

5.1 Risk Analysis

Before delving into assessing the resilience of an infrastructure system, a risk analysis gives decision makers a better understanding of:

- the types of threats the system is prone to,
- the vulnerabilities of the system,
- the consequences of system threats,
- performance measures of the system, and
- the importance of implementing resilience.

The following paragraphs provide a bird's eye view of the risk assessment procedure.

5.1.1 *Risk assessment*

As of 2006, the U.S. Department of Homeland Security (DHS) defined risk for critical infrastructure systems as a function of threat (likelihood of an attack occurring), vulnerability (relative exposure), and consequences (impact) (Masse *et al.* 2007). The risk equation is:

$$\text{Risk} = T \times V \times C, \qquad (5.1)$$

where T is the threat to the system, V is the vulnerability of the system, and C is the consequence of the threat.

However, due to the difficulty of associating a value for vulnerability across different areas, V is given a value of 1. Therefore, calculating risk involves assessing the likelihood of occurrence and the consequences. The likelihood of occurrence is a probability with a value between zero and one, while the consequences could be measured in terms of cost. The overall system risk is the sum of the individual risks.

5.1.1.1 *Threat identification*

Threats are identified by asking the question, "What could go wrong?" This is a broad question that could be answered by constructing scenarios that include the sources, causes, characteristics and targets of the threats.

A greater level of detail in the scenarios will result in less uncertainty in the risk calculation.

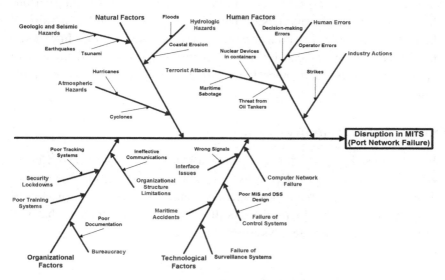

Fig. 5.1. Cause-and-effect diagram for disruption in maritime systems. Source: Mansouri *et al.* (2009b).

A cause-and-effect diagram is a useful tool that helps to identify, sort and display the possible system threats. The diagram illustrates the relationship between the sources of threats and the outcome as a result of any of those threats being realized. In the case of resilience, the threats are the causes of system disruptions. The sources of threats are human, natural, organizational and technical. Each of these factors will have secondary routes. For example, natural factors could be further divided into earthquakes, tsunamis, etc. The diagram in Fig. 5.1 shows an example of a cause-and-effect diagram that lists the sources of disruptions in the maritime infrastructure system.

The likelihood of threats is the probability of occurrence of a disruptive event. For natural disasters such as earthquakes and tornadoes, statistical methods are widely used to determine likelihood and magnitude. Human threats are harder to predict, since humans can exhibit unpredictable behavior; threats like terrorist attacks are designed to cause maximum disruption and are particularly hard to predict. As for organizational threats, it depends on the effort the organization puts into implementing processes that monitor the likelihood of the various threats. Technical threats depend partly on the quality and reliability of the technology used as well as on the operators of the system. In general, these types of threats can be predicted through statistical databases of equipment failures and other factors that contribute towards technical failures.

5.1.1.2 *Vulnerability assessment*

A widely used method for assessing vulnerability is the Swiss Cheese Model, which was developed by James Reason in 1990. The cheese slices represent the resilience schemes[1] that are already in place; the holes represent the vulnerabilities still existing in the schemes that will allow threats to penetrate the system (Fig. 5.2).

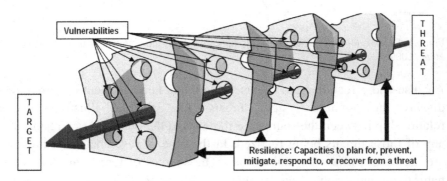

Fig. 5.2. Swiss Cheese Model for vulnerability assessment. Source: DEMA (2005).

Assessment of the vulnerabilities is a starting point for managing risk. They are an indication of the type of resilience schemes the system requires and the extent to which these schemes will be deployed.

---

[1]Resilience schemes are measures that can be taken to improve a system's resilience. Resilience in systems is achievable by reducing the vulnerability of the system to disruptions and increasing its adaptive capacity through reorganization in order for normal functionality to be resumed after the occurrence of disruptive events.

5.1.1.3 *Consequences*

Consequences are the effects of the threat on the infrastructure and on society. A consequence analysis determines if it is important to take protective measures. Although it is impossible to put a price tag on human lives, consequences are often cost-related.

A commonly used methodology for determining consequences is the cause–consequence diagram. This method is a combination of fault tree and event tree analysis. Cause–consequence analysis (CCA) identifies chains of events that can result in undesirable consequences. Fault tree analysis is used to determine the subsystem component failures and how they combine to cause system failures. Event tree analysis provides the logical representation of the possible outcomes (Isograph).

The CCA diagram represents all the system outcomes of an initial event with full textual description of the system's behavior (Andrews and Ridley 2002). The consequences include those that represent system failures as well as those that represent other system behaviors. Figure 5.3 shows the structure of a cause–consequence diagram.

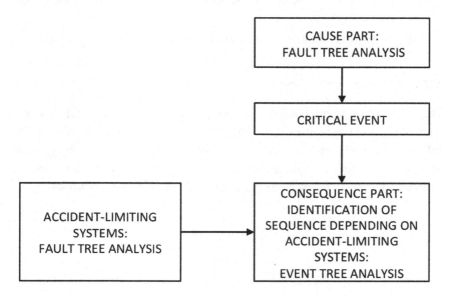

Fig. 5.3. Structure of a cause–consequence diagram. Source: Andrews *et al.* (2002).

5.2   Networked Infrastructure Resilience Assessment (NIRA) Framework

Infrastructure systems differ in their structure, value deliveries and operation. The basic structure of the proposed Networked Infrastructure Resilience Assessment (NIRA) framework can be applied to all infrastructure systems that can be represented as a network. It is important to note that the details of each step differ depending on the infrastructure system under consideration. The resilience assessment process proposed by the NIRA framework shown in Fig. 5.4 is made up of the following series of six steps:

(i)   Define the boundary of the system

(ii)   Define the resilience metrics of the system

(iii) Create a network model of the system

(iv)   Perform a resilience assessment of the system under various disruptions scenarios

(v)   Identify resilience-enabling schemes to improve the value of the resilience metrics

(vi)   Perform an evaluation of the selected resilience-enabling scheme(s)

5.2.1 *Boundary definition*

Defining the system's boundary is the first step of the NIRA framework. The system's boundaries are derived from the characteristics of the infrastructure. According to Rinaldi *et al.* (2001), infrastructure systems are spatial, operational, temporal and organizational. The NIRA framework considers the spatial, operational and temporal boundaries.

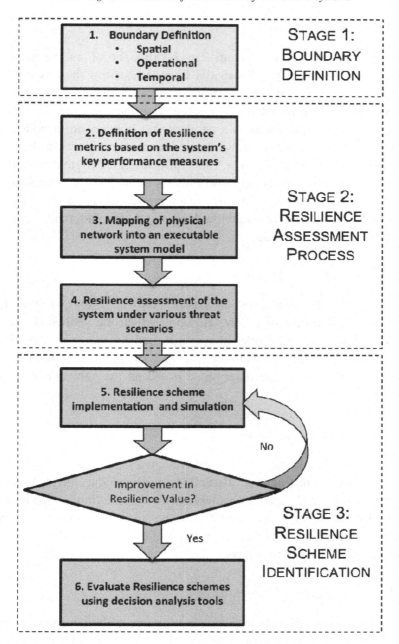

Fig. 5.4. Networked Infrastructure Resilience Assessment (NIRA) framework.

5.2.1.1 *Spatial boundaries*

The spatial scale of the system can be thought of as the physical boundary of the system. The spatial boundaries form the basis of the logical network of the infrastructure system. Although infrastructure systems differ in terms of the type of service they provide, their basic structure can be represented as a network that is made up of nodes and links. The logical network shows the connectivity relationships between the system components. For an infrastructure system such as transportation, the logical network consists of nodes that represent the cities or major junctions, while the links represent the roads. In this case, the spatial boundaries are identified by the cities and roads that the network model will include.

5.2.1.2 *Operational boundaries*

The operational boundaries determine the behavior of the key performance measures of the system upon which the resilience metrics are formulated. The network flow is specified by the operation of the infrastructure system. For example, the operational boundaries in a road transportation network are determined based on the vehicular flow per hour.

5.2.1.3 *Temporal boundaries*

The temporal boundaries define the time frame of the analysis. In a transportation infrastructure, disruptions prolong the travel time by minutes or hours. Therefore, a suitable analysis time frame is an hour or a period made up of several hours. In a maritime infrastructure system, port disruptions may hamper the port operations for more than one day. Thus, a suitable time unit is days.

5.2.1.4 *Organizational boundaries*

Organizational issues include ownership (private, public or international) and the regulatory environment. Identifying these factors become crucial for the implementation of resilience enhancement schemes.

5.2.2 *Resilience metrics definition*

The hypothesis of this research states that resilience can be measured by the impact of disruptions on the performance measures of the system, that is, the impact on the *value delivery* of the system. The resilience of the system is represented by a set of resilience values of the key performance measures that are particular to the system. These performance measures are identified by the operational boundaries of the system.

The resilience metric in a telecommunications infrastructure may be expressed based on the total amount of information (in gigabits per second) transferred between source and destination prior to and after the disruption. For a transportation network, it may be based on the increase in travel time expressed in hours. For an energy infrastructure, it may be based on the energy expressed in kilowatts per hour before and after a disruption. Also, multiple performance measures may be specified for any one system in order to obtain a more comprehensive determination of the resilience of the system.

The relationship between the value delivery of the system before and after the disruption is captured by a ratio of the two values. Therefore, the resilience metrics of the system have values that range between one and zero depending on the severity of the disruptive event. A system operating under normal operating conditions will have a resilience value of one. A resilience value of one after a disruptive event indicates that the disruption did not affect the performance of the system, as the system is still able to continue to function normally. Severe disruptions may reduce the resilience value to zero.

Disruptions impact the network nodes and/or links by reducing their capacity. Typically, it takes a certain amount of time to restore the full capacity of the nodes and links. Hence, resilience is measured for the duration of the disruptive event. It is also possible to measure resilience at a particular instance of time. Figure 5.5 shows an example of the impact of a disruptive event on the resilience value. The disruption impacts the system at time t_0 and gradually reduces the resilience metric to 0.2, with the resilience metric changing in accordance with how well the system reacts to the capacity and demand values. At time t, the resilience value goes back to one, which indicates that the system has resumed normal functionality.

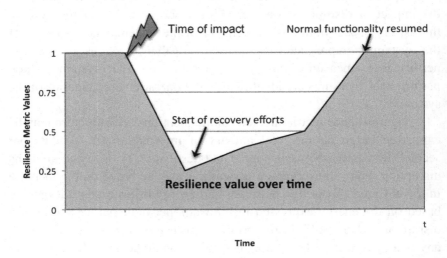

Fig. 5.5. Resilience metric values over time.

Disruptive events cause the value delivery to deteriorate. The deterioration is an increase or a decrease in the magnitude of the performance measure(s) of the system. We suggest measuring resilience over time t as shown in Eqs. (5.2) and (5.3):

$$R = \frac{\int_0^t R(t)dt}{t} \tag{5.2}$$

and

$$R(t) = \begin{cases} \dfrac{V_{after\_shock}}{V_{before\_shock}} & \text{for } \left|PM_{before\_shock}\right| > \left|PM_{after\_shock}\right|, \\[3mm] \dfrac{V_{before\_shock}}{V_{after\_shock}} & \text{for } \left|PM_{before\_shock}\right| < \left|PM_{after\_shock}\right|, \end{cases} \tag{5.3}$$

where

R	is the resilience metric,
t	is the time frame over which resilience is measured,
V_{before_shock}	is the value delivery of the system prior to a disruption,
V_{after_shock}	is the value delivery of the system following a disruption,
PM_{before_shock}	is the identified performance measure of the system prior to a disruption, and
PM_{after_shock}	is the identified performance measure of the system following a disruption.

5.2.3 *Network resilience and node-to-node resilience*

For each network, it is possible to obtain two types of resilience metrics, the *network resilience* and *node-to-node resilience*, which are elaborated upon in the following sections.

5.2.3.1 *Network resilience*

The network resilience metric reflects the impact of a disruption on one or more of the network links or nodes in the entire network. The impact of disruptions is more pronounced when it is on nodes that are more central to the network, or links that transfer heavier flows.

5.2.3.2 *Node-to-node resilience*

The node-to-node resilience reflects the impact of disruptions between any two nodes connected by a path that is made up of one or more links in the network. The disruption may be on the path connecting the two nodes or on either of the nodes at the two ends of the path. This resilience measurement is useful for assessing resilience of smaller network segments.

5.2.4 *System modeling*

There are several modeling techniques that can be used for representing networked infrastructure systems. The proposed modeling techniques for this research are network models that deploy network flow analysis theory and systems dynamics models for simulating physical networks. In some cases, a hybrid model that incorporates both network flow analysis and systems dynamics is required. Social network analysis is another modeling technique applicable to social systems (such as those at the organizational level) where the actors in the networks are the nodes and the information flow between the nodes are represented by the links.

The three parameters that are required to characterize the network are: capacity, demand and flow.

The *capacity* is determined by the flow the network is able to accommodate. The capacity of some infrastructure systems, such as transportation or telecommunication systems, refers to the links' capacity, that is, the flow that the links can accommodate. The capacity of other infrastructure systems, such as maritime transportation systems, refers to the capacity of the node to send and receive goods. The network capacity is the summation of the individual links/nodes capacities.

The *demand* is the amount of traffic that is required by one node from another node, or by one node from the rest of the network. The network demand is the demand of all the nodes in the network.

The network *flow* is the traffic that is carried over the links between the nodes of the network; it is determined by the capacity and demand data. The nature of the traffic depends on the infrastructure system. In the Internet network, it is the data carried by the fiber optic cables in gigabits per second. In a transportation network, it is the maximum number of vehicles per hour on the roads (network links) that can travel at free flow speed. It can also be defined as the kilowatt-hours of energy across the transmission lines in a power network.

Figure 5.6 shows an example of a network that consists of five nodes and seven links. Each link is bidirectional, as indicated by the arrows, and labeled by flow and capacity values (f/c). The link that connects node N_1 to node N_2 has a capacity of 10 units, whereas the link between node N_1 and N_3 has a capacity of 5 units. Node N_1 is the source node (S) and node N_5 is the destination node (T). The demand of node N_5 from node N_1 is 18 units, which are routed over the network links. The direction of flow is indicated by the dotted arrows.

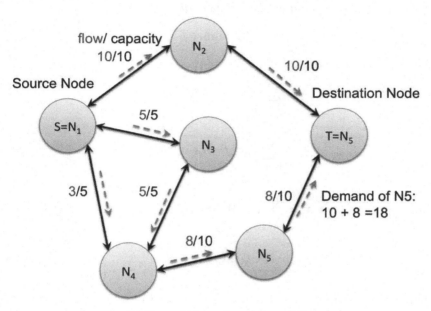

Fig. 5.6. Network demand, capacity and flow.

5.2.4.1 *System modeling using network flow analysis*

The basic operation of the physical network of an infrastructure system is to deliver flow from one point to another over the network links. The amount of flow depends on the available capacity. Severe network disruptions reduce the physical capacity of the network, thus reducing the amount of flow over the links.

Network flow analysis theorems are popular methodologies for estimating network flows. These theorems are based on the available network capacity and can be applied to model the behavior of network flow under various disruption scenarios.

The dynamics of each infrastructure system model is different. Therefore, the details of the model varies with the type of infrastructure system and the type of problems addressed. However, the basic structure of the network model is based on proven network flow analysis theorems such as the Maximum Flow Theorem.

The formulation of the Maximum Flow Theorem using linear and mixed integer programming is (Ahuja *et al.* 1993):

$$\text{Maximize } f \tag{5.4}$$

subject to the constraints

$$\sum_{j=1}^{n} x_{ij} = -f \quad \text{for} \quad i = s, \tag{5.5}$$

$$\sum_{j=1}^{n} x_{ij} = f \quad \text{for} \quad i = t, \tag{5.6}$$

$$\sum_{i=1}^{n} x_{ji} + \sum_{i=1}^{n} x_{ij} = 0 \quad \text{for} \quad \{i,j\} \in n - \{s,t\}, \tag{5.7}$$

$$0 \le x_{ij} \le c_{ij}, \tag{5.8}$$

where f is the flow, x_{ij} is the flow from node i to node j, x_{ji} is the flow from node j to node i, n is the number of nodes connected to node i, and c_{ij} is the link capacity between nodes i and j.

The above problem formulation indicates that the flow out of the source node s is equal to the flow into the destination node t; this constraint is given by Eqs. (5.5) and (5.6). Equation (5.7) is the mass balance constraint that ensures that the flow into a node is equal to the flow out of it. Equation (5.8) indicates that the flow is a positive number and that it cannot exceed the link capacity.

5.2.4.2 *System modeling using system dynamics*

System dynamics is an equation-based modeling technique that is often used for modeling infrastructure systems. System dynamics models the behavior of the system over time based on given information — for example, simulating the system under adverse conditions to evaluate whether it can meet the demand based on information such as initial storage volume, transportation capacity, and so on. The models are used to quantify consequences, and identify interdependencies within the infrastructure as well as chains of interdependencies that could create unforeseen system vulnerabilities (Brown 2006).

In system dynamics modeling, the system is represented by stocks, flows and feedback loops. The stocks represent accumulations that characterize the system and generate information upon which decisions can be made. The stocks have an inflow and an outflow, and can generate delays by accumulating the difference between the inflow and outflow. The feedback loops create the dynamics of the model. Therefore, it is the feedback loops that describe the interactions of the system. Figure 5.7 shows a simple systems dynamics model that has a stock, an inflow, an outflow and a feedback loop (Sterman 2000).

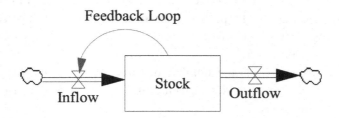

Fig. 5.7. A simple systems dynamics model.

The systems dynamics model shown in Fig. 5.7 is represented by the following integral equation:

$$\text{Stock}(t) = \int_{t_0}^{t} \left[\text{Inflow}(s) - \text{Outflow}(s) \right] ds + \text{Stock}(t_0) . \qquad (5.9)$$

System dynamics models are created using software tools such as Vensim that can graphically display and analyze models.

5.2.4.3 *System modeling using social network analysis*

Networked systems are not limited to those systems that have a physical structure for the data flow. A network can also be made up of individuals or organizations, where the network nodes are the people or the organizational entities, and the network flow is the flow between the nodes.

The birth of social network analysis (SNA) dates back to the early 19th century. It is believed that it finds its roots in the introduction of sociology as a science by Isidore Auguste Marie François Xavier Comte (1798–1857). Comte was the first scholar to propose a way of looking at societies in terms of interconnections among social actors. However, it was not until the 1970s that the Bavelas Group at Massachusetts Institute of Technology identified a formal model for centrality that formed the basis of the centrality measures used today for characterizing social networks (Freeman 2004).

Network centrality identifies the importance of the actors or nodes within the network. The four most commonly used centrality measures are degree centrality, betweenness centrality, closeness centrality, and eigenvector centrality. The performance measures that are most relevant for assessing network resilience are degree centrality and closeness centrality (Borgatti 2005).

Degree centrality is the number of direct connections that a node has. The normalized actor degree centrality C_D of node n_i in a network made up of N nodes is:

$$C_D(n_i) = \frac{d_i(n_i)}{N-1} .$$

(5.10)

Closeness centrality determines how accessible one node is to the rest of the network. In a network made up of N nodes, the closeness centrality is calculated by taking the sum of the links in each geodesic path d_G that connects node i to node j and dividing it by $N - 1$:

$$C_c(n_i) = \frac{\sum_{\substack{j=1 \\ i \neq j}} d_G(i,j)}{N-1}.$$

(5.11)

Betweenness centrality determines how often a node lies in the shortest paths between other nodes in the network. If g_{ij} is the number of geodesic paths from i to j, and g_{ikj} is the number of paths that pass through node n, then the betweenness centrality of node n is given by:

$$C_B(n) = \sum_i \sum_j \frac{g_{ij}}{g_{ikj}}. \qquad (5.12)$$

Eigenvector centrality is an indication of how important or popular a node is to the network. It is defined by the eigenvector of the adjacency matrix of the network.

Figure 5.8 is an illustration of what these centrality measures mean to the network.

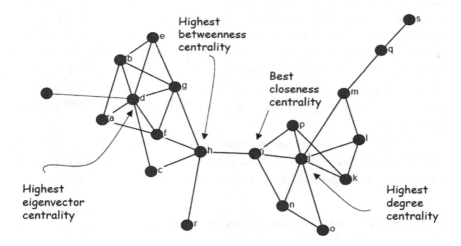

Fig. 5.8. Identifying key players in a social network. Source: Borgatti (2009).

The resilience of a node in a social network is measured by taking the ratio of the centrality measures before and after a disruption.

5.2.5 *Resilience assessment process*

The resilience assessment process involves running the models with realistic capacity and demand data in order to determine the network flow. Under normal operating conditions, the network resilience and node-to-node resilience metrics have a value of 1 — assuming that the current capacity of the network is adequate for the demand.

5.2.5.1 *Disruption scenarios*

Disruption scenarios replicate the impact of shocks on the network. The system shocks are the incidents that force the network to operate outside of its comfort zone, that is, to operate at reduced capacity or increased demand.

In order to simulate the resilience values under different operating conditions, the capacity and/or demand parameters are set to a percentage of the original values. The system model is then run using the disrupted capacity and/or demand values. Thereafter, the resilience of the system is measured based on the reaction of the system model to these disruptions by taking the ratio between the performance measures of the system before and after the introduction of the disruption. Thus, the resilience of the system is measured under various disruption scenarios that are represented by gradually reducing the capacity from 100 percent to 0 percent.

In addition to obtaining resilience metrics, the disruption scenarios help to identify the critical segments (nodes or links) in the network, and the nodes or links that suffer the most as a result of system shocks.

5.2.6 *Resilience schemes implementation and simulation*

The resilience of the system is improved by implementing one or more of the resilience-enabling schemes that were elaborated upon in more detail in Chap. 4. In a nutshell, the resilience schemes are derived from the definition of the elements that contribute to achieving resilient systems; creating a system with reduced vulnerability and enhanced adaptive capacity.

The suggested schemes for reducing the system's vulnerability (and hence make it less susceptible to disruptions) are redundancy, hardening, modularity, diversity, and capacity tolerance. The schemes for increasing the adaptive capacity to continue functionality are resource allocation, preparedness, collaboration, and cognition. The main purpose of the resilience-enabling schemes is to aid the system in coping with disruptive events.

The simulation of the resilience schemes entails adjustments to the network model so that new resilience values can be obtained.

5.2.7 *Resilience scheme evaluation*

This step of the framework determines whether it is worthwhile implementing the scheme in the physical system. The proposed methodology for resilience scheme evaluation is a three-step process that utilizes decision tree analysis, discount cash flow analysis, and cost–benefit analysis. The three steps are:

- Create a decision tree that incorporates the cost of investment in the resilience schemes under uncertainty
- Use discount cash flow analysis to evaluate the net present value (NPV) of the resilience investment on the decision tree
- Apply cost–benefit analysis to determine if the investment is worthwhile

Step 1: Create a decision tree of costs with and without a resilience scheme

Decision trees are widely used in decision analysis for choosing between several courses of action under uncertainty. Decision tree analysis (DTA) allows decision makers to decide whether to invest in resilience or not, and to choose between resilience schemes in a structured manner.

The basic structure of the resilience scheme evaluation tree is made up of a root node, chance nodes and endpoints that are linked by decision branches (Olivas 2007). Figure 5.9 shows a simple decision tree with the options to invest or not to invest in a certain resilience scheme. The root node is the starting point of the tree, from which sprout two branches that represent the decisions to invest in a resilience scheme or not. The chance nodes identify the probability of occurrence of a disruptive event. The outcome of each scheme is calculated at the endpoints, which are located at the end of the tree on the right-hand side.

The associated costs of the resilience schemes under uncertainty are the initial investment cost C_i, the operational cost C_o, and the financial losses incurred with a resilience scheme C_s. The probability of occurrence of the disruptive event is ρ, and the probability of non-occurrence is $\rho - 1$.

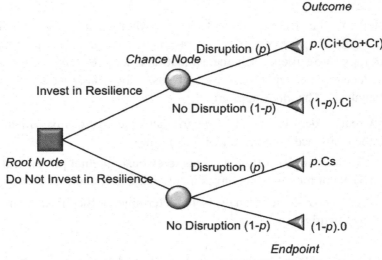

Fig. 5.9. Resilience scheme evaluation decision tree.

Implementing resilience schemes requires an initial investment cost C_i that includes implementation and maintenance costs. The schemes are only deployed in cases of disruptions so that normal functionality can be resumed. Therefore, after the occurrence of a disruptive event, there is an additional operational cost C_o that is required in order to deploy the resilience scheme.

The idea behind implementing resilience is to minimize or to eliminate the financial losses associated with disruptions. However, there may still be some losses, depending on the extent of the stakeholders' willingness to invest in a resilience scheme. Therefore, there is an additional cost C_r, which represents the financial loss incurred by the disruptive event even after the implementation of the resilience scheme(s). C_s represents the disruption costs incurred in the absence of a resilience scheme. The values of C_r and C_s are obtained by running the simulation model with the capacity and demand data under a certain disruption scenario, calculating the financial losses incurred with and without the resilience scheme.

Decision Tree Evaluation

The outcome of each decision branch is calculated by multiplying the cost of the scheme and the probabilities. The expected value of the resilience schemes is calculated at the root node starting at the right-hand side of the tree and working backwards. The expected values of the decisions to invest in resilience and not to invest in resilience are EV_{RES} and EV_{NO_RES}, respectively.

Using the above definitions of the associated costs and probabilities, EV_{RES} and EV_{NO_RES} are given by:

$$EV_{RES} = C_i + \rho(C_o + C_r) \qquad (5.13)$$

$$EV_{NO\_RES} = \rho C_s . \qquad (5.14)$$

The value of implementing resilience V_{RES} is calculated as:

$$V_{RES} = EVN_{NO\_RES} - EV_{RES} . \qquad (5.15)$$

Therefore, the value of resilience is:

$$V_{RES} = \rho(C_s - C_o - C_r) - C_i . \qquad (5.16)$$

It is also possible to choose between two or more resilience schemes in one decision tree, as shown in Fig. 5.10. The tree becomes more complicated with additional branches for more schemes. However, the evaluation principle is similar to the tree shown in Fig. 5.9.

Step 2: Use discount cash flow to determine net present value

The net present value (NPV) is a commonly used tool in finance to justify whether or not to make an investment by projecting the future income of the investment using discount rate, initial investment and projected revenues. NPV is determined by summing up the discounted cash flow C_i over a number of periods N using the discount rate (rate of return) r. The formula for NPV is given by:

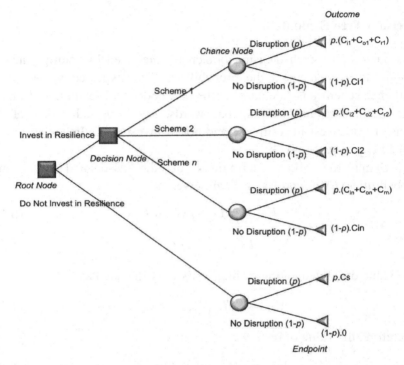

Fig. 5.10. Resilience scheme evaluation decision tree of multiple schemes.

$$NPV = \sum_{i=1}^{N} \frac{C_i}{(1+r)^i}.$$ (5.17)

An NPV value of greater than one means that it is worthwhile pursuing the investment. An NPV value of less than one indicates that the investment should not be pursued.

The NPV for a resilience scheme is calculated by replacing the cash flow C_i by the value of resilience V_{RES}. Therefore, the suggested NPV_{RES} for the evaluation of the resilience schemes over a period of time is:

$$NPV_{RES} = \sum_{i=1}^{N} \frac{V_{RES}}{(1+r)^i}.$$ (5.18)

Step 3: Cost–benefit analysis

As the name implies, cost–benefit analysis (CBA) is used to determine whether it is beneficial to implement the resilience scheme using the benefit cost ratio (BCR). A BCR value of more than one means that it is worthwhile implementing the resilience scheme. If the ratio is less than one, the resilience scheme should not be implemented. A BCR value of zero indicates that there are no advantages or disadvantages to implementing the scheme.

For resilience schemes, the benefit is NPV_{RES} and the cost is the upfront investment cost C_i. Hence, the decision rules for the cost–benefit analysis are:

$$\text{if } \begin{cases} \dfrac{NPV_{RES}}{C_i} > 1 & \Rightarrow \text{Implement} \\[2mm] \dfrac{NPV_{RES}}{C_i} < 1 & \Rightarrow \text{Do not implement} \\[2mm] \dfrac{NPV_{RES}}{C_i} = 0 & \Rightarrow \text{Indifferent} \end{cases}$$

5.3 NIRA Framework: A Systems Approach for Measuring Resilience

In an INCOSE[2] fellows' discussion that took place in February 2009, it was agreed that the systems approach for solving problems includes several key points. Some of these points, as presented by Jackson (2009), are:

- Identification of the system's elements
- Subdivision of each element into smaller elements
- Grouping of elements
- Identification of the system boundary
- Identification of the function of each element

---

[2]INCOSE is the International Council on Systems Engineering, which was founded in 1990. INCOSE's mission is to share, promote and advance systems engineering practices.

- Analysis of the interaction between elements
- Identification of the system environment
- Synthesis of the system
- Verification and validation of the system

The proposed NIRA framework adopts these guidelines for the resilience assessment process. Subdivision of systems into subsystems is a key towards infrastructure resilience assessments. A resilience assessment of an infrastructure system of systems may prove difficult or even impossible because infrastructure systems are very complex with complex interactions. Therefore, the proposed resilience assessment process is a localized process that focuses on a portion of an infrastructure system.

Subdividing infrastructure systems into smaller segments by setting appropriate boundaries makes them easier to understand and analyze. It is also important to understand the interactions between sub-segments and the interactions between the different infrastructure systems in order to predict the cascading impact of disruptions.

Infrastructure systems are synthesized as network models made up of nodes and links in order to understand the nature of the flow between the nodes. Different modeling techniques are applicable to different types of systems. While network flow analysis may be sufficient to estimate the flow of data across network cables, system dynamics models that incorporate queuing theory are required to estimate the travel time in congested traffic.

No system model is credible or complete without being verified and validated — not only to ensure that the model is a close approximation of reality and that it is functioning in the way it is supposed to function, but also to ensure that the values measured by the network model reflect the desired resilience qualities of the system. One must understand the limitation that network models can never fully represent the system, but the model should include enough data for useful information to be derived from it.

Figure 5.11 shows a schematic diagram of the NIRA framework. The diagram illustrates the assessment procedure for each step of the framework.

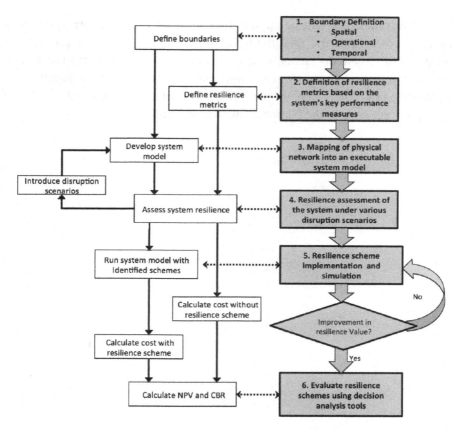

Fig. 5.11. Schematic of the NIRA framework.

5.4 Summary

In this chapter, the Networked Infrastructure Resilience Assessment (NIRA) framework was introduced. The general structure of the framework is applicable to a wide range of networked systems, with the details of each step being tailored according to the system under assessment. Although the primary foci of this book are physical infrastructure systems, the steps proposed by the NIRA framework are applicable to organizational networks as well.

The framework will be applied to a series of infrastructure systems in Chaps. 6–9. In Chaps. 6–8, the NIRA framework is applied to physical infrastructure systems, namely, the telecommunications infrastructure, the road transportation infrastructure, and the Maritime Transportation System (MTS). In Chap. 9, the NIRA framework is applied to the enterprise network of the National Intelligent Transportation System.

Chapter 6

Assessing the Resilience of the Global Internet Cable System[1]

In this chapter, the Networked Infrastructure Resilience Assessment (NIRA) framework is applied to the global Internet submarine cable infrastructure system. This case study was chosen following the 2004 Indian Ocean tsunami and the Middle East and South Asia Internet outage of 2008, which highlighted the need for incorporating resilience into the global submarine cable system. This chapter will start with a problem statement that emphasizes the underlying need for incorporating resilience. Next, an overview of the structure of the submarine cable system is presented, following which the NIRA framework is applied to measure the resilience of this infrastructure system. The application of the NIRA framework is presented in three sections: Boundary Definition, Resilience Assessment Process, and Resilience Scheme Identification. This case study will not go into the details of the decision analysis of the evaluation model.

6.1 Problem Statement

Internet traffic has become a part of everyday telecommunications, and undersea cable systems are increasingly becoming the most favored solution for global information transfer. The demand for fiber-optic cables has been increasing continuously over the past few decades (Telegeography 2005). Fiber-optic cables are considered a very reliable and secure means of data transfer, as they are harder to eavesdrop than

---

[1]Reprinted with permission from M. Omer, R. Nilchiani and A. Mostashari, *Measuring the Resilience of the Global Trans-oceanic Cable System*. Copyright (2009) IEEE.

satellites. Additionally, fiber-optic cables can be easily installed and upgraded. The trans-oceanic telecommunication cable infrastructure is made up of fiber-optic cables that lie on the ocean floor, supporting a continuously increasing demand for Internet data traffic.

Disruptions to the global fiber-optic network could result in significant commercial damage (O'Donnell 2005). Since fiber-optic cables lie on the ocean floor, they are vulnerable to various factors that could potentially cause damage. The most common damage factor is the dropping of anchors by ships, as highlighted by a major outage in the Persian Gulf in 2008 that was attributed to this factor (AP 2008). Additionally, natural disasters can also damage fiber-optic cables; The earthquake in Taiwan in 2006 caused significant damage to the Asia-Pacific undersea cables (Kitamura *et al.* 2007). Dredging fishing nets have also been reported to cause cable damage. Even marine life poses a threat, as certain species can eat their way through fiber-optic cables. Crocodile sharks damaged AT&T's first deep-sea submarine cables between the Canary Islands in 1985 (Marra 1989). Faulty equipment is another factor that can result in disruptions.

Given all the information on the vulnerabilities of submarine fiber-optic Internet infrastructure systems, there is a critical need to build resilience into this infrastructure system, which in turn creates a need for measures and metrics of resilience. Using the NIRA framework, a network model of the system is created in which hypothetical disruptions can be introduced and the effects of disruptions can be studied. The NIRA framework can provide stakeholders with the opportunity to look at different schemes that improve the system's resilience and to compare their effectiveness.

6.2 Structure of the Trans-Oceanic Cable System

In 2007, the number of global submarine cable systems exceeded 70; a number that is on the increase as demand continues to grow. Cable systems have different capacities depending on the regions they connect. The Apollo cable system, which connects North America to Europe, has a capacity of 1,400 Gbps and is considered the largest.

A fiber-optic cable (also known as optical fiber) is made up of a glass fiber core covered in cladding; a layer of buffer covers the coating to protect the fiber from damage and moisture. Information travels down the length of the glass fiber by total internal reflection.

Figure 6.1 shows a submarine cable system architecture where the undersea cable is terminated by a cable landing station at each end. The repeaters along the cable amplify and correct the signal, and the cable system transmits the signal to the terrestrial cable. Figure 6.2 shows the physical submarine cable map connecting world regions (provided by TeleGeography Research). The lines connecting the continents represent the fiber-optic cable lines.

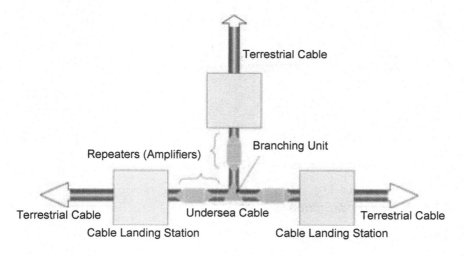

Fig. 6.1. Submarine cable system architecture. Source: *www.fsscc.org* (Pacine and Callahan 2009).

6.3   Resilience Assessment of the Global Submarine Cable Infrastructure System

In this chapter, the NIRA framework (introduced in Chap. 5), is applied to the global submarine cable infrastructure system. The framework consists of a series of steps that are grouped into the following three stages: boundary definition, the resilience assessment process, and resilience scheme identification. The following sections will elaborate on each of these stages.

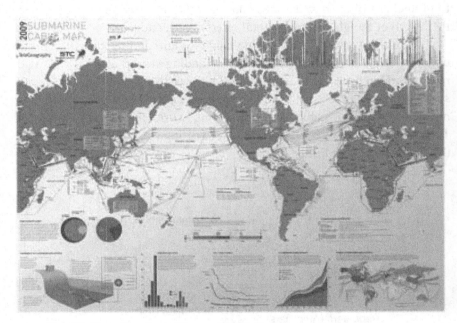

Fig. 6.2. The submarine cable map (2009). Source: *www.telegeography.com.*

6.3.1 *Boundary definition*

6.3.1.1 *Spatial boundaries*

The spatial boundaries identify the physical boundaries of the system, that is, the nodes and links in the network model. The physical network of the infrastructure system is converted into a logical network that is made up of links and nodes. The nodes represent the geographic regions, while the links are the fiber-optic cables connecting the regions.

Figure 6.3 shows the physical connections between the continents and Fig. 6.4 shows the global submarine cable infrastructure as a physical and as a logical network.

6.3.1.2 *Operational boundaries*

The behavior of the network is determined by the information flow between the nodes. Thus, the identified performance measure for this system is data transfer in gigabits per second.

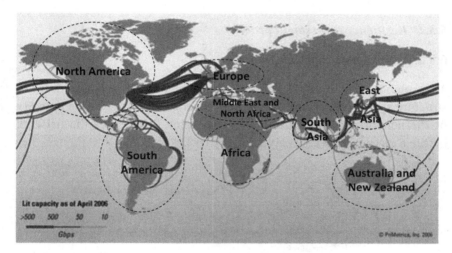

Fig. 6.3.   Physical network of the global submarine cable system. Source: *www.telegeography.com.*

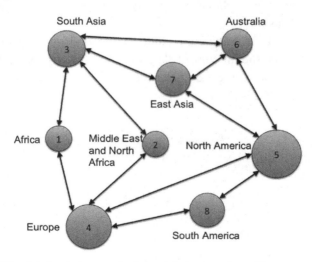

Fig. 6.4. Logical network of the global submarine cable system.

6.3.1.3 *Temporal boundaries*

The system's resilience is measured over the duration of the disruptive event. It may take several days for a submarine cable failure to be located and repaired.

6.3.2 *Resilience assessment process*

6.3.2.1 *Resilience metric definition*

The relationship for evaluating the resilience of a networked infrastructure system was defined in Chap. 5 as the ratio of the value delivery of the network after a disruption to the value delivery of the network before a disruption. This is given by Eq. (6.1):

$$
R(t) = \begin{cases} \dfrac{V_{after\_shock}}{V_{before\_shock}} & \text{for } \left|PM_{before\_shock}\right| > \left|PM_{after\_shock}\right|, \\[3mm] \dfrac{V_{before\_shock}}{V_{after\_shock}} & \text{for } \left|PM_{before\_shock}\right| < \left|PM_{after\_shock}\right|, \end{cases} \tag{6.1}
$$

where V is the value delivery of the system and PM is the identified performance measure.

Disruptions reduce the magnitude of the performance measure of the system, that is, the amount of data transfered in gigabits per second. Using Eq. (6.1), the resilience of the Internet network can be measured, as shown in Eqs. (6.2)–(6.4):

$$
R_{i\_network} = \frac{V_{after\_shock}}{V_{before\_shock}}, \tag{6.2}
$$

where

$$
V_{after\_shock} = V - V_{post} \tag{6.3}
$$

and

$$
V_{before\_shock} = V, \tag{6.4}
$$

where $R_{i\_network}$ is the resilience of the network information flow, V_{before_shock} is the initial value delivery of the Internet network and V_{after_shock} represents the value delivery of the system after the occurrence of the disruptive event. Disruption in the cable capacity results in loss of information, which in turn reduces the value delivery V. The loss in value delivery V_{loss} is the information loss as a result of cable damage.

Chapter 5 also defines the node-to-node resilience R_{node} as the ratio of the value delivery between the two nodes after a disruption to the value delivery between the two nodes before a disruption. The node-to-node resilience is measured as shown in Eqs. (6.5) and (6.6):

$$R_{i\_node} = \frac{V_{node\_after\_shock}}{V_{node\_before\_shock}} \; , \tag{6.5}$$

and therefore,

$$R_{i\_node} = \frac{V_{node} - V_{loss\_node}}{V_{node}} \; , \tag{6.6}$$

where R_{i_node} is the information flow node-to-node resilience, V_{node} is the total demand of the node, and V_{loss_node} is the total information loss (taking into consideration the information routed by the extra network capacities.) Using these resilience measures, the damage sustained when a link or a node is partially or completely down can be evaluated.

Equation (6.6) assumes a constant value delivery after the occurrence of a disruptive event. However, a system is typically repaired gradually over time. The resilience of the system over the duration of the disruptive event varies with the speed of the recovery effort. Equation (6.7) takes into account the recovery efforts until full functionality is restored:

$$R = \frac{\int_0^t R(t)dt}{t} \; , \tag{6.7}$$

where $R(t)$ is the resilience value over the time frame of the analysis t.

6.3.2.2 *System modeling*

In order to quantify the network analytically, three parameters have to be taken into consideration: node demand, link capacity, and network traffic flow.

The "demand" is the information in gigabits per second that has to be transferred from the source to the destination. The total node demand includes the total amount of information that needs to be carried through the network to the node and the internal demand of the node, that is, the information flow in the region represented by the node. The total node demand is calculated based on the total number of people in any region using the Internet and the average number of gigabits downloaded per person. Table 6.1 shows the demand figures by region as given by Internet World Stats (*www.internetworldstats.com*).

Table 6.1. Internet demand values.

Region	No. People Using Internet	Gigabits per Day	Total Demand (Gbps)
Africa	51,065,630	0.40	236
Mid East & N. Africa	41,939,200	0.56	272
South Asia	348,474,324	0.72	2,904
Europe	384,633,765	0.96	4,274
N. America	248,241,969	0.96	2,758
Australia	20,204,331	0.72	168
East Asia	230,063,933	0.72	1,917
South America	139,009,209	0.64	1,030

Table 6.2 shows the link capacity information for the model based on the values provided by TeleGeography for Internet submarine cable capacities in 2006. The capacity is measured in gigabits per second.

The links in the network are both access links and backbone links, as they are used to connect source and sink nodes as well as source or sink nodes to network nodes. For the sake of simplicity, the capacity of the link is the collective capacity of the fiber-optic cables that connect two nodes. A more realistic network model would represent each cable system by a link.

Table 6.2. Link capacities.

Link	Capacity (Gbps)
Africa – South Asia	150
Africa – Europe	120
Middle East & N. Africa – South Asia	410
Middle East & N. Africa – Europe	360
South Asia – Australia	160
South Asia – East Asia	5,190
Europe – North America	19,770
Europe – South America	160
North America – Australia	320
North America – East Asia	2,760
North America – South America	1,200
Australia – East Asia	640

The traffic flow in each link connected to a node is a percentage of the total demand of the node. For example, for the Africa node connected to South Asia and Europe, it is assumed that 30 percent of the total node demand is inside Africa, 50 percent of the demand is from South Asia and 20 percent of the total node demand is from Europe. The assumption for node demands is shown in Table 6.3.

Table 6.3. Flow in links based on percentage of total node demand.

To/ From	Africa	Middle East & N. Africa	S. Asia	Europe	N. America	Australia	E. Asia	S. America
Africa	30%	—	50%	20%	—	—	—	—
Middle East & N. Africa	—	20%	35%	45%	—	—	—	—
S. Asia	1%	10%	29%	—	—	5%	55%	—
Europe	1%	3%	—	24%	71%	—	—	1%
N. America	—	—	—	15%	60%	5%	15%	5%
Australia	—	—	1%	—	34%	64%	1%	—
E. Asia	—	—	20%	—	60%	1%	19%	—
S. America	—	—	—	5%	90%	—	—	5%

The traffic flow in the Internet network is asymmetric, as there are different upload and download rates for every region. For example, Africa might access websites hosted by Europe more than the other way around.

The asymmetrical demand ratio between any two nodes i and j is captured using the demand ratio coefficient β_{ij} given by:

$$\beta_{ij} = \frac{d_{ij}}{d_{ij} + d_{ji}} . \qquad (6.8)$$

Since β_{ij} is the ratio from node i to node j, the ratio γ_{ij} from node j to node i is given by:

$$\gamma_{ij} = 1 - \beta_{ij} , \qquad (6.9)$$

where d_{ij} is the demand of node j from node i, and d_{ji} is the demand of node i from node j.

The first step of the analysis is to calculate the amount of information that is lost when disruptions occur. The model allows hypothetical disruptions to be introduced into the network and to assess the resultant amount of information loss. The network optimization problem can thus be formulated as:

$$\text{Maximize } V \qquad (6.10)$$

subject to the constraints

$$\sum_{j=1}^{n} x_{ij} + s_i \leq D_i \text{ for } i = 1, 2, \ldots, n , \qquad (6.11)$$

$$x_{ij} = \begin{cases} d_{ij} & \text{for } \alpha_{ij} c_{ij} > d_{ij}, \\ \alpha_{ij} c_{ij} & \text{for } \alpha_{ij} c_{ij} \leq d_{ij}, \end{cases} \qquad (6.12)$$

$$x_{ij} + x_{ji} \leq \alpha_{ij} c_{ij} , \qquad (6.13)$$

$$0 \leq x_{ij} \leq c_{ij} , \qquad (6.14)$$

where

V is the total information through the network,

x_{ij} is the flow from node i to node j,

x_{ji} is the flow from node j to node i,

n is the number of nodes connected to node i,

D_i is the demand of node i,

c_{ij} is the link capacity,

s_i measures the amount of information lost when the capacity of any link is reduced (V_{loss}),

α_{ij} is the capacity degradation coefficient, and

d_{ij} is the demand of node i from j.

The flow between any two nodes is represented by x_{ij}; initially, the flow is equal to the demand d_{ij} between the two nodes. The value of the total demand for each node is given in Table 6.2, and the demand d_{ij} is based on the percentages given Table 6.3.

Equation (6.11) is the node demand constraint: the sum of the flow into one node is equal to the total demand of that node. The value of α_{ij} is used to introduce hypothetical disruptions in the form of capacity; α_{ij} is initially set to one and then gradually reduced to zero for total capacity loss. Any information that cannot reach the destination due to a capacity reduction of the link is captured by the coefficient s_i. Equation (6.12) ensures that the flow is equal to the demand if there is sufficient capacity. In the case that the capacity is sufficient, the maximum flow in the link is equal to the remaining capacity. Equation (6.13) ensures that the bidirectional flow through the link does not exceed the capacity of the link c_{ij}. Equation (6.14) sets the flow to a positive number and ensures that it does not exceed the link capacity.

The total information loss when a link is partially or fully disrupted is calculated by subtracting the value delivery after the disruption from the value delivery before the disruption as shown by:

$$V_{loss} = V - V_{post} \qquad (6.15)$$

and

$$V_{post} = \sum x_{ij} , \qquad (6.16)$$

where

V is the value delivery of the system,

V_{post} is the value delivery after capacity loss, and

x_{ij} is the flow from node i to node j.

- **Network Resilience**

For the overall network resilience, the value delivery is the total information flow in the network. The resilience is calculated using Eq. (6.2).

- **Node-to-Node Resilience**

The node-to-node resilience is the resilience between two nodes when the link between them is disrupted. It is measured as the ratio between the total information flow between the nodes after a disruption to the total information between the nodes prior to the disruption. The node-to-node resilience is calculated using Eq. (6.6).

- **Critical Link Identification**

The vulnerability of the network is evaluated by identifying the links in the network that would lead to greater damage than others when disrupted.

Some links have a much higher capacity than others and are more central to the network and hence are more critical. Identification of these links helps to identify the structural vulnerabilities of the network, and reinforcing these links would increase the whole system's resilience. These links can be identified by gradual degradation of capacity; the critical links will result in the most value loss when their capacity is reduced. The link capacity in the network model is controlled by the coefficient α_{ij}.

6.3.3 *Resilience scheme identification*

Resilience schemes aid the system to be more resilient by reducing the susceptibility of the system to disruptions (i.e., reduce vulnerability) and increasing its adaptive capacity. Figure 6.5 shows several resilience schemes that were identified in Chap. 4 — most of which are applicable to the submarine cable system. In this case study, Capacity Tolerance (Sec. 4.2.4), Resource Allocation (Sec. 4.3.1) and Redundancy (Sec. 4.2.1) are applied in order to quantify their effectiveness in improving resilience values.

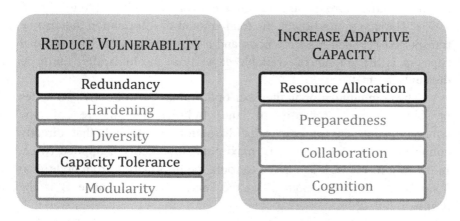

Fig. 6.5. Selected resilience-enabling schemes for the Internet submarine cable system.

The Capacity Tolerance scheme implies that the system should be designed to accommodate more than its demand limits. For the Internet cable system, this refers to the residual capacity of the cables. When a cable cut occurs in the network, the remaining link capacity may not be sufficient for the whole flow. One way to improve the resilience of the system is to use the residual capacity c_res_{ij} of the other links in the network to transfer the information between the nodes when the link between them is down. For such a scheme to be effective, Resource Allocation is also required to facilitate rerouting of network flow using the available equipment required to perform such a task in a timely manner.

Application of the Redundancy scheme entails increasing the capacity of the network by adding redundant capacity to the links in the network, and hence improving the resilience values. However, this is a costly scheme that requires planning and implementation after careful assessment of the critical links in the network.

6.3.3.1 *Resilience scheme implementation*

If a link between two nodes suffers from a capacity reduction that results in information loss, the maximum flow of the network is used to reroute the information through the residual network capacities (Ahuja *et al.* 1993). The maximum flow is the total amount of information that can be transported between a source node and a destination node. The residual capacity is the amount of available capacity in the links after the node demands are met.

The communication in the fiber-optic cables between any two nodes is bidirectional. Because of the bidirectional nature of the communication, in the case of a disruption in the link that directly connects a node A to a node B, maximum flow theory is applied twice. In the first instance, it is applied to route the information from node A to node B. In this case, node A is the source node and node B is the destination node.

Since the nature of the flow is asymmetric, the ratio of the flow between any two nodes should be kept the same as the original ratio when rerouting the information over the residual capacities of the network. This is achievable through the multiplication of the lost information V_{loss} by the demand ratio coefficients given in Eqs. (6.8) and (6.9).

Equations (6.17)–(6.22) show the network optimization problem when rerouting the information between the two nodes connected to the disrupted link:

$$\text{Maximize } \beta_{ij} V_{loss} \qquad (6.17)$$

subject to the constraints

$$\sum_{j=1}^{n} y_{ij} \leq -\beta_{ij} V_{loss} \quad \text{for } i = s , \qquad (6.18)$$

$$\sum_{j=1}^{n} y_{ij} \le \beta_{ij} V_{loss} \quad \text{for } j = t , \tag{6.19}$$

$$\sum_{i=1}^{n} y_{ji} + \sum_{i=1}^{n} y_{ij} = 0 \quad \text{for } \{i,j\} \in n -\{s,t\} , \tag{6.20}$$

$$y_{ij} \le \beta_{ij} c\_res_{ij} , \tag{6.21}$$

$$0 \le y_{ij} \le c\_res_{ij} , \tag{6.22}$$

where

V_{loss} is the amount of information lost due to the down link,

β_{ij} is the demand ratio coefficient from node A to node B,

y_{ij} is the flow from node i to node j,

y_{ji} is the flow from node j to node i,

n is the number of nodes connected to node i, and

c_res_{ij} is the residual capacity of the link.

Equations (6.18) and (6.19) determine the maximum amount of information that can be routed from the source to the destination. Equation (6.20) ensures that the total flow into a node between the source node and the destination node is equal to the total flow out of it. Equation (6.21) ensures that the flow does not exceed the allocated capacity.

In the second instance, maximum flow theory is applied to route the information from node B to node A. In this case, node B is the source and node A is the destination. V_{loss} is multiplied by the demand ratio coefficient γ_{ij} given in Eq. (6.9).

The optimization problem can then be formulated as:

$$\text{Maximize } \gamma_{ij} V_{loss} \tag{6.23}$$

subject to the constraints

$$\sum_{j=1}^{k} z_{ij} \leq -\gamma_{ij} V_{loss} \quad \text{for } i = s \ , \tag{6.24}$$

$$\sum_{j=1}^{k} z_{ij} \leq \gamma_{ij} V_{loss} \quad \text{for } j = t \ , \tag{6.25}$$

$$\sum_{i=1}^{k} z_{ji} + \sum_{i=1}^{k} z_{ij} = 0 \quad \text{for } \{i,j\} \in n \ -\{s,t\} \ , \tag{6.26}$$

$$z_{ij} \leq \gamma_{ij} c\_res_{ij} \ , \tag{6.27}$$

$$z_{ij} \geq 0 \ , \tag{6.28}$$

where

V_{loss} is the amount of information lost due to the down link,

γ_{ij} is the demand ratio coefficient from node B to node A,

z_{ij} is the flow from node i to node j,

z_{ji} is the flow from node j to node i,

k is the number of nodes connected to node i, and

c_res_{ij} is the residual capacity of the link.

Equations (6.24) and (6.25) determine the maximum amount of information that can be routed from the source to the destination. Equation (6.26) ensures that the total flow into a node between the source node and the destination node is equal to the total flow out of it. Equation (6.27) ensures that the flow in any link does not exceed the allocated capacity.

After the application of the network optimization problem specified by Eqs. (6.17)–(6.22), the total amount of information into node A is determined by:

$$V_{salvage\_a-b} = \sum_{j=1}^{n} y_{it} \ . \tag{6.29}$$

The amount of salvageable information into node B is obtainable by the application of the network optimization problem specified by Eqs. (6.23)–(6.28) as:

$$V_{salvage\_b-a} = \sum_{j=1}^{k} z_{it} \cdot \qquad (6.30)$$

The total amount of salvageable $V_{salvage}$ information between the two nodes is:

$$V_{salvage} = V_{salvage\_a-b} + V_{salvage\_b-a} \cdot \qquad (6.31)$$

The total value delivery loss when rerouting is used as a resilience scheme is:

$$V_{loss} = V - V_{post} + V_{salvage} \cdot \qquad (6.32)$$

6.3.4 *Case study results*

The optimization model specified by Eqs. (6.10)–(6.14) was programmed and simulated using Excel Solver. The capacity and demand data given in Tables 6.1 and 6.2, respectively, were used to calculate the network resilience described by Eq. (6.2).

- **Resilience Assessment**

The results showed that the resilience of the network has a value of one for all the links, which indicates that all the links in the network are able to support the total demand in its normal undisrupted state. This also indicates that the node-to-node resilience has a value of one.

Disruptions to cables caused by undersea earthquakes, fish bites or ship anchors reduce the capacity of the cable under attack, in turn resulting in a reduction of the overall link capacity. The effect of such a disruption is modeled by reducing the available link capacity using the coefficient α_{ij}. The capacity of each link, one link at a time, was reduced to 80 percent, in order to measure the impact of reducing the capacity of the individual links on the overall network resilience.

The graph in Fig. 6.6 show that reducing the capacity of the North America–South America link to 80 percent reduces the network resilience to 0.992. Reducing the capacity of the Middle East–South Asia link to 80 percent reduces the network resilience to 0.996. The rest of the links have no impact on the network resilience, as the remaining capacity of the links is able to handle the node demands.

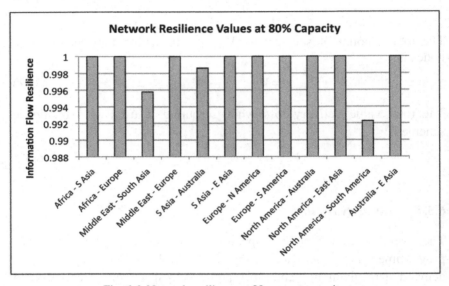

Fig. 6.6. Network resilience at 80 percent capacity.

It often takes several days or even weeks to locate and repair a faulty cable. Figure 6.7 shows an example of a disruption which reduces the capacity of the link between the Middle East and South Asia link that lasts for six days.

On the first day of the disruption, the link capacity is reduced to 40 percent of its original capacity, and it takes two days to locate the failure and begin restoration efforts. Once the failure has been located, the recovery period lasts for a total of four days.

Sixty percent of the capacity is regained by the third day after the disruption, and then the link operates at eighty percent for the last three days until full capacity is restored. Using Eq. (6.7), the resilience value for the duration of the disruptive event was calculated to be 0.68. This value means that only about 70 percent of the total information is being transmitted over the link.

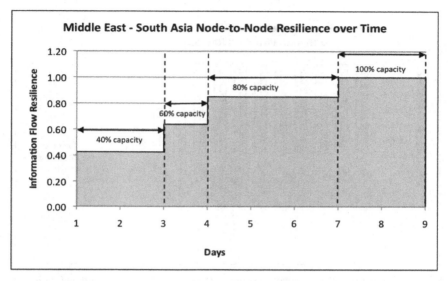

Fig. 6.7. Example of a disruptive event in the Middle East–South Asia link.

- **Resilience Schemes**

As previously mentioned, the purpose of resilience enhancement schemes is to reduce the system's vulnerability by fully utilizing the resources available to the network. Some of the links have residual capacities even after the node demands have been satisfied; these residual capacities can be used to reroute the information that would otherwise be lost.

Since the communication between any two nodes in the disrupted link is bidirectional, Eqs. (6.17)–(6.22) were used to reroute the information over the residual capacities of the other links in the network between the two nodes, in one direction; Eqs. (6.23)–(6.28) were used to route the information in the other direction. The lost information after rerouting is captured by Eqs. (6.29) and (6.30), and the network resilience and node-to-node resilience values are recalculated using Eqs. (6.2) and (6.5). Figure 6.8 shows a comparison of the resilience values for each link when the lost information is routed over the residual capacities of the network's links. It can be seen that rerouting over extra capacities increases the resilience metric value.

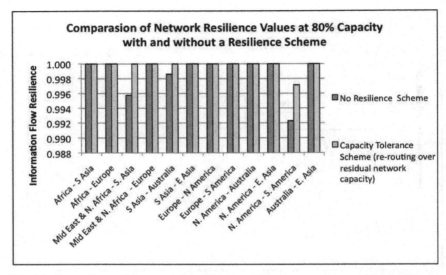

Fig. 6.8. Comparison of the network resilience at 80 percent capacity with and without a resilience scheme.

The impact of using the residual capacities of the network on resilience can be seen more clearly when a link capacity is zero, that is, completely disrupted. The graph in Fig. 6.9 shows the impact of a link at zero percent capacity on the network resilience when the lost information is rerouted over the residual network capacities. It can be seen from Fig. 6.9 that reducing the Capacity of the Europe–North America link or the South Asia–East Asia link to zero has a huge impact on the network resilience.

The rerouting capabilities of the network are only as good as the rerouting capability of the link with the least capacity. The addition of redundant capacities to the links that create these bottlenecks will result in a dramatic increase in the amount of information that the network is able to reroute, which will in turn further improve the network's resilience. Additionally, depending on the severity of the disruption, the amount of information loss could be beyond the rerouting capabilities of the network. It should also be noted that rerouting over residual capacities might increase the time it takes for the information to be delivered from the source to the destination.

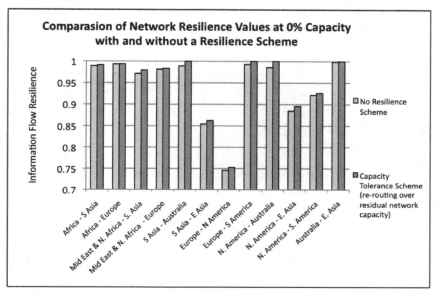

Fig. 6.9. Network resilience at zero percent capacity with and without a resilience scheme.

Node-to-node resiliencies measure the resilience between any two nodes in the network. In the disruption profile shown in Fig. 6.10, the resilience of the Middle East–South Asia link is reduced by 30 percent. Applying the Capacity Tolerance scheme, which entails rerouting over residual capacities, increases the resilience value from 0.68 to 0.82, which is almost 15 percent. This is an indication that the residual capacity can carry about 15 percent of the information that would otherwise be lost. Figure 6.10 shows the improvement in resilience values as a result of rerouting.

The results obtained from the resilience analysis for the duration of the disruptive event are a clear indication that the network lacks sufficient capacity to continue normal operation. Another option for improving the resilience value is to add redundant capacities to the links that may cause a bottleneck in the network. In this case, adding redundant capacity to the Middle East & North Africa–Europe link,

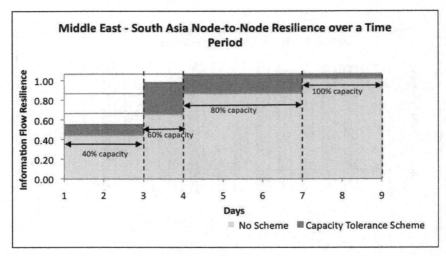

Fig. 6.10. Resilience of the Middle East–South Asia link with and without a resilience scheme.

which is a link in the rerouting path, helps to maintain a resilience value of one even if the Middle East & North Africa–Europe link is completely destroyed. Figure 6.11 shows the node-to-node resilience of the Middle East & North Africa–South Asia link.

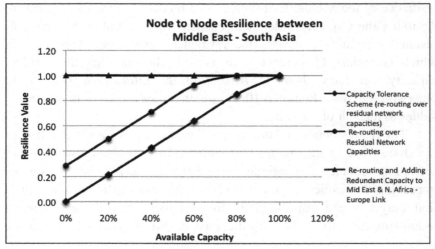

Fig. 6.11. Node-to-node resilience between the Middle East and North Africa and South Asia.

6.4 Summary

Recent events such as the undersea cable disruptions near Alexandria (Egypt) in 2008 and the Indian Ocean tsunami in 2004 have highlighted the vulnerability of the global undersea cable infrastructure. Analyzing and implementing resilience into an infrastructure system is a way of mitigating the consequences of such disruptions as well as preparing the infrastructure system in the face of these threats.

In this chapter, the NIRA framework was applied to the global Internet submarine cable system. It was demonstrated that link disruptions reduce the capacity of the links, which in turn impacts the key performance parameters of the system. For this particular system, the identified key performance measure is the data flow in the fiber-optic cables measured in gigabits per second.

Application of schemes such as Capacity Tolerance (that utilizes the residual capacity of the network to reroute information) allows the system to continue to function and improves resilience values. The application of this scheme depends on the available physical capabilities of the system. The case study also showed that adding redundant capacity to some of the links in the network that cause bottlenecks improves the resilience value.

So far, we have looked into the network resilience when a link is partially or fully disconnected. Future studies should investigate the impact of a node being partially disrupted, and the impact of the disruption on the whole network. Other redundancy schemes call for the use of parallel systems such as satellites to transmit the data to improve resilience. This is, of course, only achievable if the system has the option of using diverse systems recommended by the Diversity scheme.

Chapter 7

Assessing the Resilience of Road Transportation Networks

In this chapter, the NIRA Framework is applied to two road transportation networks. In the first case study, the NIRA framework is applied to the road network that connects Boston to New York City, and the impact of disruptions on the major arterials connecting these two cities is investigated. The resilience of this road network is characterized in terms of delays, environmental damage and financial losses. Since there are several transportation alternatives between Boston and New York City, the case study investigates the impact of disruptions on the traveler's mode of choice.

In the second case study, the NIRA framework is applied to the island of Manhattan's entry-points road network. In this case study, different resilience-enabling schemes are evaluated through the use of decision tree analysis.

7.1 Problem Statement

The transportation infrastructure is particularly vulnerable to environmental hazards such as heavy snowstorms or floods that temporarily immobilize functionality whilst causing structural damage. Additionally, the transportation system itself is a source of hazard; accidents caused under the influence of drugs, by speeding, or by fatigue are daily incidents. Advanced vehicle technology, clever road designs, the punishment of erring drivers, and driver awareness programs can help to decrease the probability of accidents substantially.

Other sources of disruptions are road works or mechanical failures that result in the collapse of bridges and tunnels. Disruptions not only lead to substantial travel delays but also to the loss of human lives (Astaneh-Asla 2008) and substantial financial losses. Tilahun and Levinson (2007) studied the economic impact of the collapse of the I-35W in Minnesota in 2007. The collapse resulted in economic losses of US$17 million and US$43 million in 2007 and 2008 respectively (DOT 2009).

A resilient infrastructure is less susceptible to disruptions and is able to recover from natural and man-made disasters with minimum losses. Creating resilience in transportation networks limits the socio-economic losses due to disruptions. Thus, metrics are needed to assess the current resilience of these networks and to evaluate the effectiveness of resilience-enabling schemes.

7.2   Resilience Assessment of Boston–New York Corridor

The NIRA framework is made up of three stages and each stage is composed of a series of steps. The three stages are: boundary definition, resilience assessment process, and resilience scheme identification. The following sections will elaborate on each on these stages in detail.

7.2.1   *Boundary definition*

The boundaries defined by the NIRA framework are the spatial boundaries, the operational boundaries, and the temporal boundaries.

7.2.1.1   *Spatial boundaries*

The physical network is a representation of the roads that connect the major cities between Boston and New York City. In addition to Boston and New York City, the cities included in the physical network are Providence, Brockton, Springfield, Worcester, New Haven, Bridgeport, Stamford and Hartford. Figure 7.1 shows the road network that connects these cities. The network shown in Fig. 7.1 can be mapped as a directed logical network, as shown in Fig. 7.2.

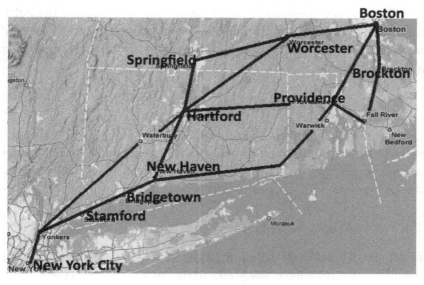

Fig. 7.1. The Boston–New York road transportation network.

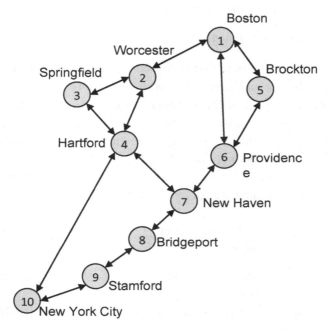

Fig. 7.2. Logical network of the Boston–New York transportation corridor.

The cities are the nodes of the network and the roads are the links. The resultant logical network is made up of 10 nodes and 13 directed links. For the sake of simplicity, only the major roads have been taken into consideration.

7.2.1.2 *Operational boundaries*

The type of network flow determines the operational boundaries. The operation of road transportation networks is governed by the vehicular movements on the roads. The vehicular movement is measured in vehicles per hour.

7.2.1.3 *Temporal boundaries*

The temporal boundaries define the time frame of the analysis. In this case study, the resilience is assessed over the period of one day.

7.2.2 *Resilience assessment process*

7.2.2.1 *Resilience metric definition*

In Chap. 5, we derived the relationship between the value delivery levels of the system before and after a disruptive event. Disruptions often cause the value delivery level of the system to deteriorate. The severity of the deterioration depends on the severity of the disruptions, as well as how well the system is able to cope based on the physical capacity of the nodes and links in the network. The relationship shown in Eq. (7.1) describes the resilience metrics based on the type of performance measure that defines the value delivery of the system.

$$R(t) = \begin{cases} \dfrac{V_{after\_shock}}{V_{before\_shock}} & \text{for } |PM_{before\_shock}| > |PM_{after\_shock}|, \\[2ex] \dfrac{V_{before\_shock}}{V_{after\_shock}} & \text{for } |PM_{before\_shock}| < |PM_{after\_shock}|, \end{cases} \tag{7.1}$$

where V is the value delivery of the system and PM is the identified performance measure.

The definitions of the performance measures for this network are based on Foster's definition of the resilience aspects in transportation networks (Foster 1997). He defines different principles of resilience including social, economic, environmental, systemic, timing and physical resilience. Every system will have a different degree of resilience with respect to each of these aspects. Based on this definition, we identify three performance measures for this road network: travel time, environmental impact, and cost.

- **Travel Time Resilience**

A disruptive event in the road network reduces the capacity of the road, that is, the maximum number of vehicles that can use the facility under prevailing conditions, which will in turn result in a prolonged travel time. Under normal operating conditions, the travel time resilience has a value of one. A disruptive event may cause an increase in travel time between two nodes, thereby making the resilience value approach zero.

Equation (7.2) gives the resilience metric with regard to travel time. The resilience value is an indication of how the disruption affects the system. A value of 0.5 means that the travel time is doubled as a result of the disruptive event. A resilience value of zero indicates that it is impossible to travel between the two nodes through the disrupted route.

$$R_{tt} = \frac{t_{i,j \ (before \ shock)}}{t_{i,j \ (after \ shock)}} \ , \tag{7.2}$$

where R_{tt} is the travel time resilience, and t_{ij} is the travel time between node i and node j.

There may be more than one route connecting the two nodes. In the case of Boston to New York, six alternative routes have been identified. The travel time between Boston and New York is calculated as the average travel time of all the routes.

- **Environmental Resilience**

The prolonged travel time caused by disruptive events increases the overall network fuel consumption, which in turn increases the level of

CO_2 emissions. The environmental resilience metric is based on the environmental impact as a result of the increased level of CO_2 emissions.

The environmental impact is measured as the product of CO_2 emissions per gallon, and the number of gallons consumed during the trip. The CO_2 emissions from gasoline is estimated by the Environmental Protection Agency to be 19.4 pounds per gallon (USEPA 2005). Fuel consumption is based on a model developed by Emmerson (2007) that takes into account the distance traveled, the delay, and the number of stops and starts during the travel time. Equations (7.3) and (7.4) are used to calculate the environmental impact and the environmental resilience, respectively:

$$Env\_Impact = \begin{array}{c} CO_2 \text{ Emissions per Gallon of Fuel} \\ \times \text{ No. of Gallons Consumed} \end{array}, \quad (7.3)$$

$$R_{ENV} = \frac{Env\_Impact_{before\_shock}}{Env\_Impact_{after\_shock}}. \quad (7.4)$$

The resilience will have a value of one in the absence of delays in the network and approaches zero as the travel time between two nodes increases to infinity.

- **Cost Resilience**

The associated financial cost due to delays includes the extra cost due to the additional time taken, the cost of fuel, and the cost of mitigating the environmental impact of increased CO_2 emissions. The cost associated with time varies according to the individual, the type of work they do, and whether the trip is for business or leisure. It is assumed here that the average cost per hour per person is US$12; this figure is based on approximate average wages. Statistical analysis of road users may give a better approximation. The cost resilience is given by:

$$R_{Cost} = \frac{Cost_{before\_shock}}{Cost_{after\_shock}}. \quad (7.5)$$

7.2.2.2 *System modeling*

Analytical quantification of the network requires knowledge of the demand and capacity of the network. The capacity and demand data determine the flow that is used to calculate the travel time.

The network "demand" is the total number of vehicles per hour traveling from Boston to New York City. There are several ways of estimating the demand — such as intercity trip generation and modal choice, as well as available highway traffic statistics. The demand is estimated using aggregate datasets provided by the Massachusetts Highway Department (MASSDOT 2007) for routes originating in Boston.

The total demand of the network *D* is the sum of all the demands of the individual cities (nodes), which is approximately 9,650 vehicles per hour. It should be noted that this figure represents a grossly oversimplified approximation; better intercity travel demand models would provide a more accurate figure. However, the focus here is the assessment of resilience, while the travel demand is a given input into the optimization problem.

The "highway capacity" is based on the 2000 Highway Capacity Manual (HCM 2000). The capacity for each segment is 2,400 passenger cars per hour per lane, and this figure was adjusted to include truck traffic to 3,500 vehicles per hour per highway.

A disruption in the road network will result in delays that increase the travel time. Therefore, the network optimization problem is to minimize the average travel time between Boston and New York City. The segment travel time between any two nodes is calculated using the Bureau of Public Roads (BPR) function (Horowitz 1991), as shown in Eq. (7.5), but can be substituted with any flow–speed or flow–travel time relationship such as that proposed by Akçelik (1991) or Skabardonis and Dowling (1997). The BPR function shown in Eq. (7.6) is the most commonly used relationship for estimating travel speed due to increasing in travel volumes:

$$t_{ij} = \frac{l_{ij}}{55(\text{mph})} \left[1 + 0.15 \left(\frac{x_{ij}}{c_{ij}} \right)^4 \right], \qquad (7.6)$$

where

t_{ij} is the time it takes to travel between node i and node j,

l_{ij} is the length of the link between node i and node j,

x_{ij} is the flow between node i and node j, and

c_{ij} is the capacity of the link between node i and node j.

Several routes or paths have been identified between Boston and New York City. These are:

P_1:   Boston, Worcester, Hartford, New York City.

P_2:   Boston, Worcester, Springfield, Hartford, New York City.

P_3:   Boston, Brockton, Providence, New Haven, Bridgeport, Stamford, New York City.

P_4:   Boston, Providence, New Haven, Bridgeport, Stamford, New York City.

P_5:   Boston, Worcester, Hartford, New Haven, Bridgeport, Stamford, New York City.

P_6:   Boston, Worcester, Springfield, Hartford, New Haven, Bridgeport, Stamford, New York City.

The travel time for each route is calculated by summing up the travel time t_{ij} of all the links along the path. For example, the travel time for P_1 is given by:

$$P_1 \text{ Travel Time} = \sum_{i=1}^{n-1} t_{ij} \quad \text{for } \{i, j\} \in P_1 , \tag{7.7}$$

where

P_1 is a route between Boston and New York City,

t_{ij} is the time it takes to travel between node i and node j, and

N is the number of nodes on P_1.

The travel time between Boston and New York City is measured as the average travel time Avg_tt_{st} of all the routes connecting the source to the destination node. The average time is given by:

$$Avg\_tt_{st} = \frac{\sum_{i=1}^{k} P_i}{k} , \tag{7.8}$$

where

Avg_tt_{st} is the average travel time between source s and destination t,

P_i is a route between Boston and New York City, and

K is the number of routes connecting Boston and New York City.

The network optimization problem determines the flow based on the total demand, which is the summation of all the vehicles per hour traveling between the nodes. It is assumed that the flow between Boston and New York City is equal to the total demand. In addition to the demand, the network optimization problem takes into account the links' capacities and segment travel times.

The network optimization problem is given by Eqs. (7.9)–(7.16).

$$\text{Minimize } Avg\_tt_{st} \tag{7.9}$$

subject to the constraints

$$\sum_{i=1}^{n} x_{sj} = D , \tag{7.10}$$

$$\sum_{i=1}^{n} x_{ij} + \sum_{j=1}^{n} x_{ji} = 0 \text{ for } \{i, j\} \in n - \{s, t\}, \tag{7.11}$$

$$\sum_{i=1}^{n} x_{it} = D , \tag{7.12}$$

$$C_{ij} \leq \alpha_{ij} c_{ij} , \tag{7.13}$$

$$D = \beta_{ij} D_{norm} , \tag{7.14}$$

$$t_{ij} = \frac{l_{ij}}{55(\text{mph})} \left[1 + 0.15 \left(\frac{x_{ij}}{c_{ij}} \right)^4 \right] , \tag{7.15}$$

$$x_{ij} \geq 0 , \tag{7.16}$$

where

Avg_tt_{st} is the average travel time for all the routes between the source s and destination t,

D_{norm} is the network demand under normal operating conditions,

D is the actual demand of the network,

x_{sj} is the flow out of the source node,

x_{ij} is the flow into a node in the network,

x_{ji} is the flow out of a node in the network,

x_{it} is the flow into the destination node,

co_{ij} is the original link capacity,

c_{ij} is the link capacity after a disruption,

α_{ij} is the capacity degradation coefficient,

β_{ij} is the demand increase coefficient, and

n is the number of links connected to a node.

Equation (7.10) ensures that the flow exiting from the source node (Boston) is equal to the demand of the network, which is the total number of vehicles traveling out of Boston. Equation (7.11) sets the mass balance constraint, that is, the flow into the nodes between the source and destination nodes is equal to the flow out of the node. Equation (7.12) ensures that the flow reaches the destination node (New York City).

The capacity of the link can be degraded to zero using the capacity degradation coefficient α_{ij} given in Eq. (7.13). The segment travel time in Eq. (7.14) increases as a result of the capacity reduction. In addition to decreasing the link capacities, it is possible to investigate the behavior of the network under different demand values by adjusting β_{ij} in Eq. (7.15). The adjustment of α_{ij} and β_{ij} are discussed in more detail in the following section. The flow is a positive value, a constraint that is given by Eq. (7.16).

- **Disruption Scenarios**

The network resilience is evaluated by assessing the impact of capacity reduction (of the network links). For this transportation network, the links are the highways that connect the major cities between Boston and New York City. The capacities of the road segments are specified by the maximum number of vehicles that are able to travel at the free-flowing speeds permitted on the road segments.

Disruptions such as accidents result in the blockage of some of the highway lanes, and as a result, the maximum number of vehicles that are able to travel at free-flowing speed is reduced. The number of vehicles specified by the demand is constant, and this constant demand coupled with reduced highway capacity will cause congestion and consequently travel time delays.

Disruptions on the road segments are modeled by varying the coefficient α_{ij} given in Eq. (7.12). If the value of α_{ij} is set to one, the links will operate at full capacity. A value of 0.4 will reduce the link capacity by 60 percent; this means that only one out of the three highway lanes are in operation. Total road blockage can be modeled by setting the value of α_{ij} to zero. Similarly, the increase in load is modeled by increasing the demand value using the coefficient β_{ij} as given by Eq. (7.13). Setting the value of β_{ij} to one means that the network is operating under normal demand conditions; setting the value of β_{ij} to more than one increases the demand.

- **Critical Link Identification**

The model is used to evaluate the impact of link disruption on the resilience values. The critical links in the network are those that have the severest consequences, which include prolonged travel time, negative environmental impact, as well as the highest financial losses. These financial losses include the extra costs associated with the additional time taken, the additional fuel consumption and CO_2 mitigation.

7.2.3 Resilience scheme identification

Chapter 4 identified several schemes that improve the resilience of systems. The schemes were organized into two categories. Those in the first category reduce the vulnerability of the system, while those in the second increase its adaptive capacity.

For this particular network, the applicable vulnerability reduction schemes are Redundancy (Sec. 4.2.1), Diversity (Sec. 4.2.3) and Capacity Tolerance (Sec. 4.2.4). The Cognition scheme increases the adaptive capacity of the system. The above-mentioned schemes are highlighted in Fig. 7.3.

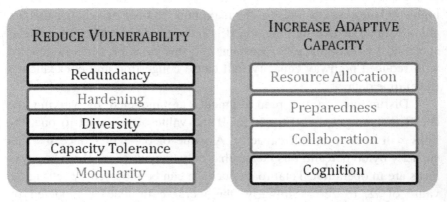

Fig. 7.3. Resilience-enabling schemes for the Boston–New York city corridor.

In road transportation networks, physical redundancy entails the construction of parallel roadway systems, which is unrealistic and costly. The recommended redundancy is functional redundancy, where parallel systems such as rail and air are deployed. The Diversity scheme facilitates functional redundancy by providing the parallel systems that provide functional redundancy.

Capacity Tolerance is another scheme that is applicable to road transportation networks. It implies that the capacity of the roads should accommodate more than the regular demand. However, this scheme is only effective in the short term. In reality, the availability of extra road capacities encourages more travelers to use the road networks, hence increasing the demand.

The Cognition scheme (Sec. 4.3.4) entails the application of intelligent solutions based on the current and predicted states of the system, where the user is continuously informed about the current state of the network.

• Mode Choice Analysis

Mode choice analysis is used to determine the most preferred mode of transport among the available options between Boston and New York City, which are auto (cars and buses), rail and air. Change in demand affects travelers' mode choice. The analysis is based on level of service (LOS) variables such as the Wait Time (t_w), Access Time (t_a), Travel Time (t_t), Cost (C) and Comfort (H) (Sussman 2000).

Our assumption is that the *base case,* with regards to the LOS under normal operating conditions, is by car. Normal operating conditions imply full operating capacity and regular demand values. The mode choice for each of the transportation modes is determined against the base case using the utility of the traveler's choice given by:

$$U\_mode = \frac{\dfrac{a_1}{Time} + \dfrac{a_2}{Cost} + \dfrac{Comfort}{a_3}}{3}, \qquad (7.17)$$

where

a_1, a_2, a_3 are the base case LOS coefficients,

Time   is the total transport time of the mode (sum of travel time, wait time and access time),

Cost   is the cost of the trip of the transport mode, and

Comfort   is the comfort level of the transport mode.

Comfort is measured as a function of travel time, wait time, access time and cost; an increase in the total transport time reduces comfort. Equation (7.17) determines the utility functions U_{auto}, U_{train} and U_{air} for auto, train and air, respectively. The utility functions are used to calculate the probability of the number of passengers choosing one of the available transport modes:

$$P(auto) = \frac{U_{auto}}{U_{auto} + U_{train} + U_{air}} \,, \tag{7.18}$$

$$P(train) = \frac{U_{train}}{U_{auto} + U_{train} + U_{air}} \,, \tag{7.19}$$

$$P(air) = \frac{U_{air}}{U_{auto} + U_{train} + U_{air}} \,. \tag{7.20}$$

7.2.4 Case study results

The optimization model was programmed in Microsoft Excel and the program Solver was used to execute the model. Equations (7.9)–(7.16) were applied to determine the flow under normal operating conditions in order to obtain a value for the average travel time Avg_tt_{st} from Eq. (7.8) between Boston and New York City. The average travel time was calculated to be approximately six hours.

The resilience metrics reflect how the system responds to shock or disruptions. Under normal operating conditions, the system's resilience has a value of one; this value approaches zero as the system becomes incapable of coping with the disruption. In order to measure the system's resilience metrics, hypothetical disruptions in the form of link capacity reductions were introduced into the network model by adjusting the coefficient α_{ij} from Eq. (7.13). Equation (7.2) was then used to calculate the travel time resilience. Figure 7.4 shows the impact on the network travel time resilience of reducing the capacity of each link by 60 percent.

The resilience value reflects the impact of a disruption on the journey time from Boston to New York City; lower resilience values indicate longer travel times. The results show that reducing the capacity of certain links in the network reduced the resilience value, while reducing the capacity in others has little or no impact.

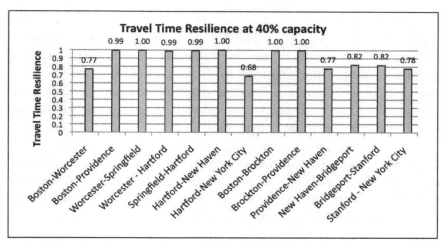

Fig. 7.4. Travel time resilience at 40 percent link capacity.

Vehicles traveling from Boston to New York City have the option of traveling through Worcester, Brockton or Providence. As the link between Boston and Worcester lies on the shortest path, it is a preferred route. Reducing the capacity of that link to 40 percent significantly impacts journey time. A resilience value of 0.77 implies that there is an increase in travel time of more than 20 percent.

On the other hand, reducing the capacity of either Boston–Brockton or Boston–Providence does not impact the resilience values, because vehicles prefer to travel via Worcester since the capacity of this link can accommodate the flow sufficiently. It is important to note that a limited number of vehicles travel over the disrupted links as long as the capacity is not exceeded.

Figure 7.4 shows that the travel time resilience value of the journey between Boston and New York City remains one when Worcester–Springfield or Worcester–Hartford is reduced to 40 percent, which means that the disruption does not impact the journey time between Boston and New York City. This is due to the availability of an alternative route, Worcester–Hartford. The same logic applies for the Worcester–Hartford link: the vehicles traveling out of Worcester have the option of traveling to Springfield and then to Hartford instead of traveling directly from Worcester to Hartford, without a significant increase in travel time.

The link between Hartford and New York City has the lowest resilience value. This implies that this link is one of the critical links in the network. In addition to this link belonging to the shortest path, the alternative route from Hartford to New York City does not have sufficient capacity to accommodate the flow without increasing the journey time. The resilience is reduced to 0.68, which implies that the travel time increases by more than 30 percent.

When a disruption occurs, fuel consumption increases due to the prolonged travel time. This in turn increases CO_2 emissions and results in a greater impact on the environment. Figure 7.5 shows the environmental resilience when link capacity is reduced to 40 percent. The environmental resilience is calculated by using Eq. (7.4).

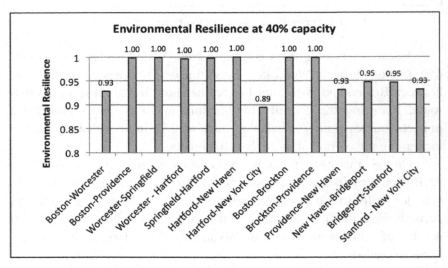

Fig. 7.5. Environmental resilience at 40 percent link capacity.

As expected, the Hartford–New York City link causes the most environmental damage when operating at 40 percent capacity. The results show that this capacity reduction reduces the environmental resilience to 0.89; that is, the environmental impact increases by more than 10 percent. Although vehicles cause environmental damage in the form of CO_2 emissions, the calculations assume the environmental resilience to have a value of one under normal operating conditions.

A more accurate environmental resilience measurement would include the impact of the vehicles on the environment when the network is operating at full capacity.

Figure 7.6 shows the estimated financial losses per day for the Hartford–New York City link when operating at capacities of less than 100 percent. The corresponding cost resilience metrics are shown in Fig. 7.7.

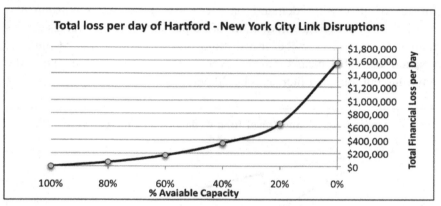

Fig. 7.6. Total financial loss per day versus percent available capacity.

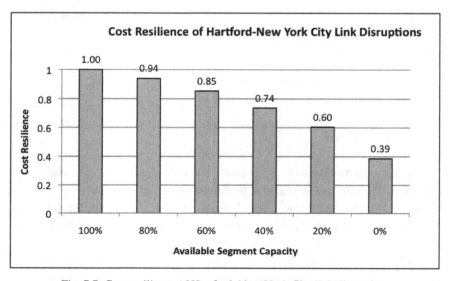

Fig. 7.7. Cost resilience of Hartford–New York City link disruption.

The losses include the cost of extra fuel consumed, the loss of time, and the cost of CO_2 mitigation. Even a reduction of just 20 percent will incur a financial loss of more than US$50,000 per day. This number increases dramatically with the reduction in capacity. The estimated losses are more than US$1.5 million if the link is completely disrupted.

An increase in demand can occur due to an event at a certain venue or due to road obstructions in adjacent networks. Figure 7.8 shows the impact of increasing demand on the travel time and environmental resiliencies. An increase in demand of 50 percent results in values of less than 0.5 and 0.8 for the travel time and environmental resiliences, respectively. This means that the average travel time doubles while the environmental impact increases by 20 percent.

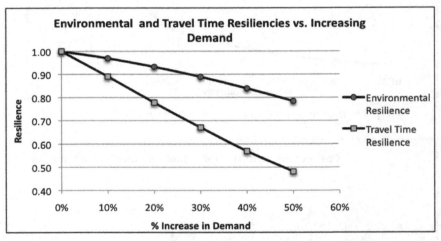

Fig. 7.8. Impact of 50 percent demand increase on travel time resilience and environmental resilience.

Road disruptions also impact travelers' choices of mode of transport. It is assumed that the preferred mode of transport for the trip between Boston and New York City is by car. A disruption prolongs travel time, which increases the total transportation time and cost as well as decreases the comfort.

Figure 7.9 shows how the probabilities of the different mode choices change with capacity reduction. It is assumed that under normal operating conditions, the most favorable mode of transport is by car. The probabilities are calculated using Eqs. (7.18)–(7.20).

The weights of the LOS variables — travel time, wait time, access time, and cost – were set to 3, 0.5, 1, and 4, respectively. The values are selected based on a scale that varies from 0 to 5 in increments of 0.5, where 0 is the least significant and 5 is the most significant. The above weights indicate that the system's users value cost as the highest criteria, followed by travel time, then access time. The weights also show that travel time is three times more important than access time, and that cost is four times more important that access time. The LOS of the least concern is the waiting time. The weights of the LOS variables are subjective values and can be adjusted according to the users. The purpose of this example is to demonstrate the impact disruption on mode-choice given the above-mentioned weight assignment.

As link capacity decreases, more and more passengers will choose to travel by rail or air. Figure 7.9 shows that when the capacity of the link between New Hartford and New York City is at 15 percent, most travelers will opt to take the train or go by air.

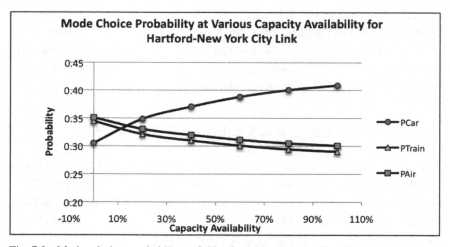

Fig. 7.9. Mode choice probability of Hartford–New York City link under various disruptive scenarios.

7.2.5 *Case study conclusion*

Road obstructions often occur due to accidents, roadwork, or even natural causes such as snowstorms. The capacity of the road is determined by the maximum number of vehicles traveling on the road under normal traffic conditions. A reduction in capacity or an increase in the network demand will result in delays that produce negative environmental and financial impacts.

In this case study, we analyzed the impact of disruptions on travel time resilience, environmental resilience and cost resilience metrics. We identified the links in the network that cause the maximum delays and result in severe environmental and financial losses. Additionally, we investigated the impact of delays on mode choice with regard to the level of service (LOS) variables. Our results show that prolonged road travel time will divert the mode choice from cars to other available forms of transport such as rail or air.

Our findings so far focused on the vulnerability aspect of resilience and investigated the consequence of network vulnerability. Future studies will be carried out to evaluate the impact of implementing vulnerability reduction schemes such as increasing the capacity of existing links, the addition of extra routes and reducing recovery time. Future research will also address the aspect of adaptive capacity that promotes resilience, that will allow the network to reorganize in order resume normal functionality with minimum losses.

7.3 Resilience Assessment of Manhattan's Points of Entry

The island of Manhattan in New York is home to more than 1.6 million people. Since it is the business and commercial center of New York City, the number of people in Manhattan swells to more than four million people during the day. Figure 7.10 shows the daytime population of Manhattan versus that at night (after business hours).

Although a significant number of travelers opt for public transport, the bridges and tunnels that connect Manhattan still carry an average of 90,000 vehicles per hour in both directions. The only vehicular access to Manhattan is through various tunnels and bridges, and the transportation of goods (such as food) is primarily by the use of trucks via these tunnels and bridges.

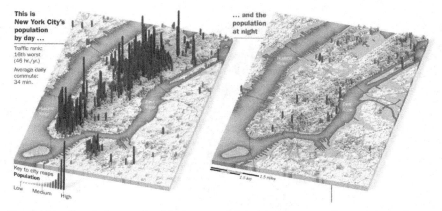

Fig. 7.10. Population of Manhattan by day versus by night. Source: *www.urbanomnibus.net* (Slobin 2009).

This case study emphasizes the importance of incorporating resilience in busy regions where all the access points are either on or under water. Evaluating the resilience of Manhattan's points of entry is carried out by applying the methodology proposed by the NIRA framework. The following sections will elaborate on each of the main stages of the framework: boundary definition, resilience assessment process, and resilience scheme identification.

7.3.1 *Boundary definition*

7.3.1.1 *Spatial boundaries*

The physical boundary of the network model includes the bridges and tunnels that connect Manhattan to the outside world as well as the road network that links the entry points outside the island. Figure 7.11 shows the main bridges and tunnels that connect Manhattan. For the sake of simplicity, the smaller East Harlem River bridges have not been taken into consideration. Figure 7.12 shows the corresponding logical network, which is made up of 14 nodes and 25 directed links. The nodes in the network represent the area connected to Manhattan via the entry points.

The network links represent the bridges and tunnels that lead to Manhattan as well as the major intersections that connect the roads.

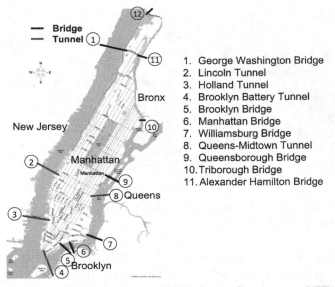

1. George Washington Bridge
2. Lincoln Tunnel
3. Holland Tunnel
4. Brooklyn Battery Tunnel
5. Brooklyn Bridge
6. Manhattan Bridge
7. Williamsburg Bridge
8. Queens-Midtown Tunnel
9. Queensborough Bridge
10. Triborough Bridge
11. Alexander Hamilton Bridge

Fig. 7.11. Main entry points to the island of Manhattan. Source: *www.iNETours.com.*

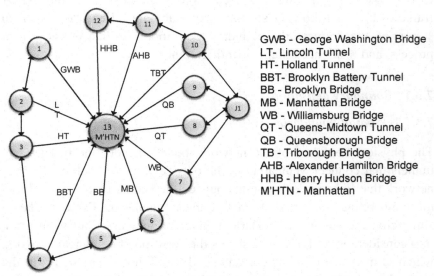

GWB - George Washington Bridge
LT- Lincoln Tunnel
HT- Holland Tunnel
BBT- Brooklyn Battery Tunnel
BB - Brooklyn Bridge
MB - Manhattan Bridge
WB - Williamsburg Bridge
QT - Queens-Midtown Tunnel
QB - Queensborough Bridge
TB - Triborough Bridge
AHB -Alexander Hamilton Bridge
HHB - Henry Hudson Bridge
M'HTN - Manhattan

Fig. 7.12. Logical network of Manhattan's main entry points.

7.3.1.2 *Operational boundaries*

The type of network flow determines the operational boundaries. In this case, the operational boundaries are the vehicular movements along the roadway. Vehicular movement incorporates both truck and car traffic.

7.3.1.3 *Temporal boundaries*

Disruptions often last for several hours or even days, depending on the severity of the disruption and the speed of the recovery and restoration effort. For this network, the resilience is measured over the period between 7am and 10pm; the time frame representing the busiest period of the day.

7.3.2 Resilience assessment process

7.3.2.1 *Resilience metric definition*

The risks that threaten this infrastructure system such as roadwork, floods, accident or mechanical failures – which could result in the collapse of the entry points — will result in prolonged travel times. Therefore, the network travel time was identified as the resilience metric of the system. The goal of this study is to measure the resilience of the tunnels and bridges that connect Manhattan. Hence, the analysis is focused on the system's node-to-node resilience.

The *node-to-node travel time resilience* R_{t_ij} given in Eq. (7.21) is derived from Eq. (7.1). It is measured as the ratio of the travel time between the two nodes i and j preceding a disruption to the travel time between the two nodes following a disruption.

$$R_{t\_ij} = \frac{t_{ij(before\_shock)}}{t_{ij(after\_shock)}}, \tag{7.21}$$

where

t_{ij} is the travel time from node i to node j.

The node-to-node resilience over a specified time period (t) is measured using:

$$R_{t\_node} = \frac{\int_0^t R_{t\_ij(t)dt}}{t} . \tag{7.22}$$

Using this resilience metric, it is possible to evaluate the damage when a link is partially or completely disrupted. The resilience has a value of one under normal network operations and approaches zero as travel time increases to infinity.

7.3.2.2   System modeling

As with the previous case study, the network model requires the demand and capacity data in order to determine the flow, and subsequently, the travel time. The network demand for this network is the total number of vehicles per hour traveling into Manhattan via the bridges, as well as the regular traffic on the roads connecting the entry points. The demand is based on statistics provided by the New York State Department of Transportation (NYSDOT) (Sadik-Khan 2007) and State of New Jersey Department of Transportation (NJDOT).

The links in the network represent different types of roads. The highway capacity is based on the 2000 Highway Capacity Manual (HCM 2000). The calculations take into account the speed limits imposed on the highways and arterials that make up the network, as well as truck and heavy vehicle traffic. It should be noted that these travel demand and capacity figures represent a grossly oversimplified approximation; more accurate figures can be obtained by using intercity demand models.

The network flow is the number of vehicles per hour traveling into Manhattan in addition to the number of vehicles per hour traveling in the rest of the network links. The optimal flows of the network can be calculated by minimizing total network travel time — provided that the demand is met. The segment travel time between any two nodes is calculated using the Bureau of Public Roads (BPR) function developed by Horowitz (1991). The function given in Eq. (7.23) is also used to measures the travel time in congested traffic.

$$t_{ij} = \frac{l_{ij}}{\text{free flow speed (mph)}} \left[1 + 0.15 \left(\frac{x_{ij}}{c_{ij}} \right)^4 \right], \tag{7.23}$$

where

t_{ij} is the time it takes to travel between node i and node j,

l_{ij} is the length of the link between node i and node j,

x_{ij} is the flow between node i and node j, and

c_{ij} is the capacity of the link between node i and node j.

The capacity of the road segments was calculated using the Base Capacity formula shown in Eq. (7.24) given by the Highway Performance Policy Manual (HPPM 2000).

$$BaseCap = 1,000 + 20 FFS, \tag{7.24}$$

where *FFS* is the free flow speed. The base capacity was adjusted to accommodate truck traffic by multiplying it by a factor of 0.2. This factor was obtained using the heavy vehicle coefficient f_{HV} assuming that 15 percent of the vehicles are trucks. The f_{HV} is given by:

$$f_{HV} = \frac{1}{1 + P_T (E_T - 1)}, \tag{7.25}$$

where P_T is the proportion of trucks and buses in the traffic stream and E_T is the passenger-car equivalent, which is 1.5 for all urban highways.

The objective function is to minimize the travel time of all the links in the network. The network optimization problem is shown in Eqs. (7.26)–(7.34):

$$\text{Minimize } t_n \tag{7.26}$$

subject to the constraints

$$\sum_{j=1}^{n} x_{sj} = D_s, \tag{7.27}$$

$$\sum_{i=1}^{n} x_{ij} + \sum_{j=1}^{n} x_{ji} = 0 ,$$
(7.28)

$$\sum_{i=1}^{n} x_{it} = D_s ,$$
(7.29)

$$z_{ij} = x_{ij} + D_{ij} \quad \text{for } i \neq s ,$$
(7.30)

$$c_{ij} = \alpha_{ij} c_{ij} ,$$
(7.31)

$$t_{ij} = \frac{l_{ij}}{\text{free flow speed (mph)}} \left[1 + 0.15 \left(\frac{x_{ij}}{c_{ij}} \right)^4 \right] ,$$
(7.32)

$$t_n = \frac{\sum_{i=1}^{n} \sum_{j=1}^{n} D_{ij} t_{ij}}{\sum_{i=1}^{n} \sum_{j=1}^{n} D_{ij}} ,$$
(7.33)

$$x_{ij} \geq 0,$$
(7.34)

where

t_n is the network travel time,

D_s is the demand on the disrupted link,

x_{sj} is the flow out of the source node,

x_{ij} is the flow into a node in the network carrying the demand of the disrupted link,

x_{ji} is the flow out of a node in the network carrying the demand of the disrupted link,

x_{it} is the flow into the destination node (Manhattan),

c_{ij} is the link capacity before the disruption,

C_{ij} is the link capacity after the disruption,

α_{ij} is the capacity degradation coefficient,

z_{ij} is the network flow after the disruption,

l_{ij} is the length of the segment between node i and node j,

t_{ij} is the time it takes to travel from node i to node j,

D_{ij} is the demand from node i to node j, and

N is the number of links connected to a node.

Equation (7.27) ensures that the flow exiting from the source node (end of a disrupted bridge outside of Manhattan) is equal to the demand between the disrupted bridge and the destination (Manhattan). Equation (7.28) sets the mass balance constraint; that is, the flow into the nodes between the source and destination nodes is equal to the flow out of the node. Equation (7.29) ensures that the flow reaches the destination node (Manhattan). Equation (7.30) is the final flow of the network, which includes the regular traffic in the network in addition to the traffic between the source and the destination. Equation (7.31) determines the current capacity of the links in the network through the adjustment of coefficient α_{ij}. Equation (7.32) is the BPR function for calculating travel time. Equation (7.33) calculates the average network travel time. Equation (7.34) expresses the constraint that the flow is a positive value.

- **Disruption Scenarios**

In road networks, the road capacity is given by the maximum number of vehicles that are able to travel at the free-flowing speed specified by the road segment. Disruptions reduce that number and result in delays if the number of vehicles on the road is more than the specified capacity. The impact of capacity reduction can be modeled by introducing hypothetical disruptions using the coefficient α_{ij} given by Eq. (7.29). The network links operate at full capacity through setting the value of α_{ij} to one. A value of 0.5 will reduce the link capacity by 50 percent, while a value of 0.3 reduces the link capacity to 30 percent, and so on. Total road blockage can be modeled by setting the value of α_{ij} to zero.

Resilience over a prolonged time period can be calculated by including the effect of demand values taking into account peak and off-peak traffic throughout the day.

7.3.3 Resilience scheme identification

7.3.3.1 Resilience scheme options

Resilience is achievable by taking proactive measures prior to a disruption, and reactive measures preceding a disruption. Proactive measures are implemented prior to disruptive events and reduce the susceptibility of the system to disruptions, thereby making the system less vulnerable. Reactive measures take place after the occurrence of the disruptive event, allowing the system to continue to function with minimum losses.

One of the vulnerability-reducing schemes identified in Chap. 4 is Diversity (Sec. 4.2.3). The Diversity scheme entails the deployment of parallel systems such as ferries and trains in cases of severe disruptions. Ferries are frequently used as a mode of transport to and from Manhattan; they were also used as an escape route when the World Trade Center was attacked in 2001 (Pyle 2006). In the cases of severe disruptions, ferries that would otherwise transport goods can be converted to carry passengers. An unused fleet of passenger ferries can also provide an efficient commute between the source and the destination.

Another resilience-enabling scheme identified in Chap. 4 is Cognition (Sec. 4.3.4). This scheme enhances the reactive resilience measures of the system and hence increases its adaptive capacity. Cognition in transportation networks is achievable through the use of an intelligent transport system that measures the demand and volume in the network and recommends alternative routes whilst minimizing travel time delays.

7.3.3.2 Resilience scheme evaluation

Implementation of the above-mentioned schemes requires a structured decision analysis process by which decision makers can choose between alternative schemes and also to evaluate their cost effectiveness. Decision tree analysis is a commonly used tool to calculate the expected value of the alternatives under uncertainty.

Figure 7.13 shows the decision tree of the expected outcomes with and without a resilience scheme. If the probability of the occurrence of the disruptive event is ρ, the probability of non-occurrence is $\rho - 1$. In the case of a disruptive event, implementation of the resilience scheme has the following associated costs: the cost of the investment C_i, the operational cost C_o, and the financial loss incurred with the resilience scheme due to the disruptive event C_r. If no resilience scheme is implemented and a disruption occurs, the financial loss due to the disruption is C_s.

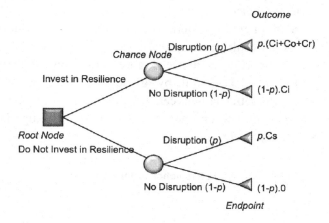

Fig. 7.13. Decision tree for evaluating resilience schemes.

The decision tree is used to calculate the net present value NPV_{RES} at the decision node over a number of N periods using the discount rate (rate of return) r:

$$NPV_{RES} = \sum_{i=1}^{N} \frac{\rho(C_s - C_o - C_r) - C_i}{(1+r)^i}. \qquad (7.35)$$

It is worth pursuing the implementation of the resilience scheme if the value of NPV_{RES} is higher than the investment cost C_i.

7.3.4 *Case study results*

7.3.4.1 *Resilience assessment*

The methodology of the NIRA process was applied to the bridges and tunnels that connect New York City to Manhattan. The model was programmed in Microsoft Excel and the program Solver was used to execute the model. Equations (7.26)–(7.34) were applied to determine the flow, to introduce a hypothetical disruption into the model, and to calculate the network travel time. Equation (7.22) was used to determine the node-to-node resilience.

Under normal operating conditions, the resilience value is one. Capacity disruptions result in an increase in travel time, which reduces the value of the network's resilience. Figure 7.14 shows the impact of reducing the capacity of each link by 40 percent on the node-to-node resiliencies during peak traffic between 4pm and 7pm. A reduction of 40 percent occurs frequently when one lane of a tunnel or bridge is closed due to repairs, accidents, etc.

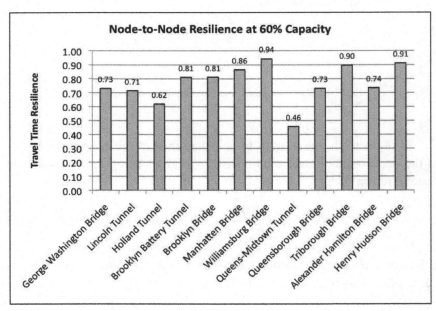

Fig. 7.14. Node-to-node travel time resilience at 60 percent capacity.

The results indicate that, with its current capacity, the network is vulnerable to disruptions. In some cases, such as the Holland Tunnel, the capacity reduction results in a resilience value of 0.6, which implies that the travel time increases by 40 percent. The linear relationship between the capacity reduction and demand increase in the Holland Tunnel link indicates that the Holland Tunnel is operating at its capacity limits.

One vulnerability reduction scheme is to route the traffic over the other links in the network. With prior knowledge of the disruption, vehicles traveling into Manhattan through the Holland Tunnel will choose to travel over other entry points. Figure 7.15 shows a comparison of the node-to-node resilience values with and without a vulnerability reduction scheme.

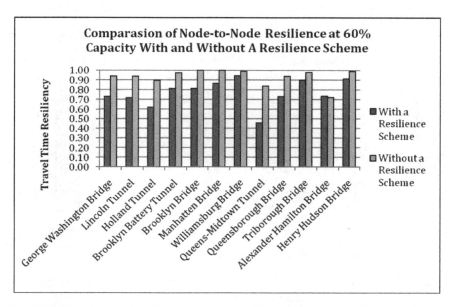

Fig. 7.15. Node-to-node travel time resilience at 60 percent capacity with and without a resilience scheme.

Rerouting the vehicles over other routes in the network improved the node-to-node resiliencies in most cases. The Alexander Hamilton Bridge resilience value is slightly less than that without a rerouting scheme, because routing the vehicles through other routes will cause traffic congestion elsewhere, which will consequently increase the travel time in other network links.

The network demands are higher during rush hour periods such as 7am to 10 am and 4pm to 7pm than during off-peak periods. The node-to-node resilience of the Holland Tunnel was simulated to investigate the impact of these demand variations on the resilience value. The network was simulated over a 15-hour time period for the respective demand values (7am to 10am, 10am to 1pm, 1pm to 4pm, 4pm to 7pm, and 7pm to 10pm). The results are shown in Fig. 7.16. It is assumed that the vehicular traffic for each time period remains constant over the individual hourly intervals. The node-to-node resilience over this period of time is 0.64. This indicates that with the reduction in capacity, the network performance with respect to travel time is reduced by a third.

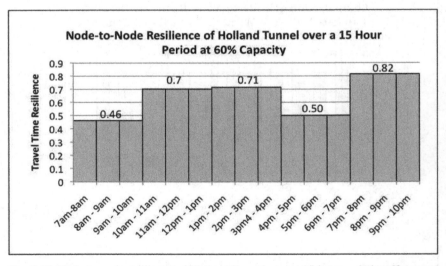

Fig. 7.16. Node-to-node resilience of Holland Tunnel over a 15-hour period at 60 percent capacity.

7.3.4.2 *Resilience scheme evaluation*

Severe disruptions in tunnels due to mechanical failures may take weeks to repair. Thus, it may be beneficial to have an alternative mode of transport available, such as ferries. This is particularly true for the location of the Holland Tunnel, since there are a fewer bridges and tunnels offering access to Manhattan on the western side of the island.

One option for evaluating schemes that improve resilience is using decision trees in combination with cash flow theory, as given by Eq. (7.35). The costs associated with the resilience scheme are: the initial investment cost C_i, the operational cost C_o, the cost incurred with the resilience scheme C_r and the cost incurred due to the disruption without a resilience scheme C_s.

Roadwork or accidents on highways alter the behavior of traffic patterns and increase fuel consumption as vehicles consume more fuel when traffic is congested. For our purposes, we use the figures for city fuel consumption given by the Environmental Protection Agency, which are 28 mpg for passenger cars and 16 mpg for light trucks (USEPA 2000), and we assume that 15 percent of vehicles are light trucks. Based on various sources, it is assumed that the dollar amount to reverse the damage caused by CO_2 emissions per gallon of fuel is US$0.013. The cost of time is set to an average value of US$12 per hour for each vehicle on the road based on the average hourly wage. Ferries reduce the number of vehicles on the road by offering an alternative mode of transport, which reduces the demand on tunnels and bridges. The value of C_r is obtained by running the simulation model using the original demand value. C_s is obtained by adjusting the demand value and rerunning the simulation model.

It was assumed that the initial investment cost C_i of converting ferries to transport half the passengers is US$300,000, the operational cost C_o is US$20,000, and that the ferries will transport 30 percent of the travelers crossing the Holland Tunnel. The analysis showed that the scheme is worth investing in for repair work that lasts more than five days, or if this type of disruption occurs more than five times within one year. It is important to note that the selected values for evaluating the resilience schemes are not intended to obtain accurate figures for the cost of resilience but rather to demonstrate the evaluation procedure.

7.3.5 *Case study conclusion*

The population of the island of Manhattan increases by more than 250 percent during the day. This fact underlines the importance of the transportation networks that connect Manhattan to the rest of the region. Due to the large number of people traveling in and out of Manhattan every day, road obstructions at Manhattan's entry points result in delays as well as negative environmental and financial impacts.

In this case study, we applied the NIRA framework to assess the node-to-node resilience of Manhattan's entry points. In the first part of the analysis, the node-to-node resilience of all the entry points was assessed. The second part of the analysis used decision trees analysis and cash flow theory to evaluate the effectiveness of offering an alternative mode of transportation such as ferries to relieve congestion in the Holland Tunnel.

7.4 Summary

In this chapter, the NIRA framework was applied to two case studies. It was first applied to assess the *network resilience* of the major arterials in the Boston–New York Corridor, and then to assess the *node-to-node resilience* of the road network associated with the points of entry into the island of Manhattan.

In general, resilience is achievable through the application of proactive and reactive measures that reduce the vulnerability of the system and increase its adaptive capacity. Capacity Tolerance is a resilience scheme that reduces the vulnerability of the system. Roads with sufficient capacity margins improve the resilience value following a disruptive event, since vehicles in the network can take alternative routes with less congestion. However, with the increase in demand along those arterials, the original travel time tends to increase. This increases the overall network travel time, which reduces the system's resilience.

Diversity is another scheme that reduces the system's vulnerability by making available alternative means of transport. Improving the service level of parallel systems such as ferries and trains will affect the choice of mode of travel by increasing the probability that more travelers utilize these parallel systems.

Traditional decision analysis tools may be applied to help decision makers with prior knowledge of the initial investment and operational costs, identify the effectiveness of various resilience schemes that can be deployed in cases of emergency.

Chapter 8

Assessing the Resilience of Maritime Transportation Systems

In this chapter, the NIRA framework is applied to the maritime transportation system (MTS). The chapter begins with an overview of the sources of disruption that can affect the MTS and describes several maritime disruptions that have occurred in recent years. The NIRA framework is then applied to the maritime transportation network that connects the main ports in East Asia and North America. The resilience of this system is assessed from a multi-metric perspective that characterizes the resilience of MTSs. The chapter attempts to quantify the impact of port collaboration in improving network resilience.

8.1 Problem Statement

MTSs play a vital role in the US economy and in the creation of jobs. In 2006, it was reported that port activities contributed two trillion dollars to the US economy — 14 percent of GDP — creating employment opportunities for more than 8 million people (Wright 2009).

Prior to September 11, MTSs were mostly focused on the safety and efficiency of the waterways (Clancy 2009). After the attacks, there were numerous discussions on the vulnerability of ports and waterways; a shift of focus from maritime safety to security. Incorporating resilience in this infrastructure system not only promotes security and reduces the susceptibility of the infrastructure to man-made and natural disruptions; it also allows these systems to apply the appropriate response and recovery measures that will enable them to continue to deliver the expected service.

Ports are extremely vulnerable to many types of hazards. Their geographical location makes them perfect targets for terrorist attacks launched outside of the port's country. It also increases their susceptibility to all kinds of natural hazards such as hurricanes and tornadoes. Given the numbers and sizes of vessels entering a large port every hour, accidents such as vessel collisions can also hinder a port's operation. Such disruptions can result in negative impacts on the US economy.

In recent years many of the world's ports suffered disruptions that affected national economies. In 1995, the Hyogo-ken Nanbu Earthquake in Kobe, Japan required the diversion of more than a hundred ships; the quake caused economic losses estimated at US$50–100 billion (Lingamfelter 2009; McCormick *et al.* 2008). The 11-day worker's strike on the west coast of the US in 2002 cost up to US$2 billion a day (Lingamfelter 2009). In 2005, the US witnessed the devastating effects of hurricane force winds when Katarina destroyed a third of the port of New Orleans, which reduced the number of ships entering the port by 50 percent (Mostashari 2008).

In 2008, the port of Houston-Galveston on the Gulf Coast suffered major disruptions caused by Hurricane Gustav, followed two weeks later by Hurricane Ike. The estimated damage per day was US$322 million (Wright 2009). Also in 2008, an oil spill on the Mississippi River following a ship collision affected both the Port of South Louisiana and Port of New Orleans. It was estimated that if the Mississippi River had been closed for a longer period of time, the cost would have approached US$275 million per day (Lingamfelter 2009).

From the above examples, it is evident that disruptions in the MTS are costly and can have a significant global economic impact. Implementing resilience in this system will reduce the negative economic impact of disruptions and prepare the system in the face of potential threats.

8.2 Resilience Assessment of Main Pacific Ports

The resilience assessment process utilizes a network model that includes the biggest ports on both sides of the Pacific Ocean as well as information about the tonnage flow between the ports. Hypothetical disruptions are imposed on the network model in terms of the port's capacity to process goods. The network model is used to identify the critical links in the network as well as to test the effectiveness of the resilience schemes.

To begin the resilience assessment, the system boundaries are defined. The boundaries are identified in terms of the physical system (spatial boundary), the type of operations (operational boundary), and the duration of the assessment (temporal boundary). The following sections will give a description of each.

8.2.1 Boundary definition

8.2.1.1 Spatial boundaries

The network model is based on ports facing the Pacific Ocean, which is one of the four major maritime circulation routes. The other routes are the Atlantic Ocean, the Indian Ocean, and the Mediterranean Sea. The Pacific Ocean carries 15 percent of global maritime trade. Ships carrying goods and passengers travel across the ocean on certain maritime routes that link the ports. The maritime routes are a few kilometers wide, with certain wind, current and weather patterns that permit ships to sail; they also have clear political borders.

Figure 8.1 shows a map of the waterways across the four oceans (Rodrigue *et al.* 2009). The methodology proposed by the NIRA framework entails obtaining a logical network from the physical network shown in Fig. 8.1. The nodes in the logical network represent the ports, and the links are the waterways that exist between the ports. The logical network includes most of the biggest ports in East Asia and the biggest ports in North America, namely: Busan (Korea), Hong Kong (China), Kaohsiung (Taiwan), Shanghai (China) Yokohoma (Japan), Seattle/ Tacoma (US), Oakland (US) and Los Angeles/Long Beach (US). Other smaller ports have not been included in the network model for the sake of simplicity. The logical network is shown in Fig. 8.2.

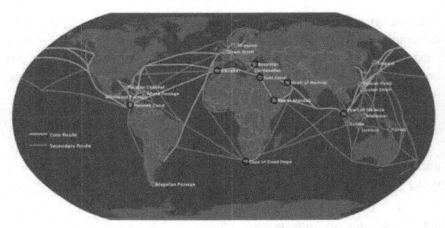

Source: Rodrigue, J-P et al. (2009) The Geography of Transport Systems, Hofstra
University, Department of Global Studies & Geography, http://people.hofstra.edu/geotrans

Fig. 8.1. Map of global maritime routes.

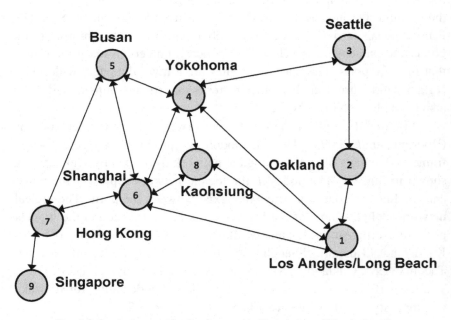

Fig. 8.2. Logical network of main ports in East Asia and North America.

8.2.1.2 *Operational boundaries*

The network flow determines the operational boundaries of this system. For this network, the flow is represented by the flow of goods between the ports in metric tons.

8.2.1.3 *Temporal boundaries*

The resilience is assessed for the duration of the disruptive event. Disruptive events in ports often last several days. Thus, the resilience is assessed for the period of days until the port recovers full operational capability.

8.2.2 *Resilience assessment process*

8.2.2.1 *Resilience metric definition*

A resilient system is one that is able to absorb system shocks and recover from a disruption so that it can resume regular operation. For infrastructure systems, a disruptive event can potentially hamper the ability of the system to continue to function. Resilience metrics measure the effect of the disruptive event on the system's performance and the ability of the system to continue to operate.

In Chap. 5, it was proposed that the resilience metrics are defined in terms of the performance measure of the system. Disruptive events cause the value delivery to deteriorate; the deterioration may either increase or decrease the magnitude of the value delivery of the system. Equation (8.1) shows the resilience metrics for both scenarios:

$$R(t) = \begin{cases} \dfrac{V_{after\_shock}}{V_{before\_shock}} & \text{for } \left|PM_{before\_shock}\right| > \left|PM_{after\_shock}\right|, \\ \dfrac{V_{before\_shock}}{V_{after\_shock}} & \text{for } \left|PM_{before\_shock}\right| < \left|PM_{after\_shock}\right|, \end{cases} \qquad (8.1)$$

where V is the value delivery of the system and PM is the performance measure that identifies the value delivery.

The resilience metric has a value of one under normal operating conditions. A disruptive event that impedes the system's performance reduces that value depending on its severity. The lowest possible resilience value is zero, which indicates a lack of resilience in the system.

Most systems have one or more metrics that measure the system's performance. In MTSs, a disruption not only limits the capability of a port to send and receive goods but also increases the time and cost to transport goods from source to destination. The questions often posed by shippers are as follows:

- Is the port able to receive the goods?
- How long it will take?
- How much will it cost?

Based on these questions, the value deliveries of the system are identified to be: tonnage resilience, time resilience, and cost resilience. Tonnage resilience reflects the ability of the system to reliably receive/send goods; time resilience represents the impact of disruptions on the time it takes to send/receive goods; and cost resilience reflects the impact of disruption on transportation costs. The following sections will address these three resilience metrics in more detail.

- **Tonnage Resilience**

A disruptive event will reduce the freight throughput capability of the port, thus limiting the physical capacity of the port to send and receive goods. Measuring this resilience metric requires knowledge of the tonnage processing capability of the port in tons and the tonnage flow in and out of the port. A port disruption can last for several days; the tonnage resilience for imports is therefore measured for the duration of the disruptive event, as given by Eqs. (8.2)–(8.4). Similar equations can be used to determine the tonnage capacity resilience for exports.

$$R_{Tn} = \frac{Tn_{after\_shock}}{Tn_{before\_shock}} \; , \qquad (8.2)$$

$$R_{Tn} = \frac{Tn_{init} \times t_{total}}{\sum\limits_{i=1}^{n} Tn_i t_i} \; , \qquad (8.3)$$

$$t_{total=}\sum_{i=1}^{n}t_i \ , \tag{8.4}$$

where

Tn_{before_shock}	is the port tonnage processing capacity before a disruption,
Tn_{after_shock}	is the port tonnage processing capacity following a disruption,
Tn_{init}	is the tonnage the port is capable of handling under normal operating conditions,
t_{total}	is the duration of the disruptive event,
Tn_i	is the tonnage during time period i,
t_i	is a time period during the disruptive event, and
n	is the number of time periods in a disruptive event.

- **Shipping Time Resilience**

Shipping time represents the sum of the travel time and wait time. A reduction in the freight processing capability of the port reduces the number of vessels that can be processed at any one time, and hence prolongs the shipping time. The shipping time's resilience can be formulated as:

$$R_T = \frac{T_{before\_shock}}{T_{after\_shock}} \ , \tag{8.5}$$

where

T_{before_shock}	is the time to transport goods between ports under normal conditions
T_{after_shock}	is the time to transport goods between ports after a disruptive event

- **Cost Resilience**

The value of the goods being transported in dollars depends on the type of goods transported. While a disruption that lasts a few days may not hugely impact the cost of goods such as cars, the same disruption will cause dramatic value depreciations in perishable goods, where time is critical. The considered transportation costs include the depreciation of the value of goods during the transportation as well as the cost of bunker fuel per mile-ton. Additionally, there are overhead costs, which include administration, security, scans, customs, and so on. A disruption will increase the overall shipping cost; the cost resilience metrics can be calculated as shown in Eqs. (8.6)–(8.9):

$$R_C = \frac{C_{init}}{C_{init} + C_{loss}} \; , \tag{8.6}$$

$$C_{loss} = c_{vd} + c_t + c_o \; , \tag{8.7}$$

$$c_{vd} = V_{cargo} \times \%V_{dp} \times d \; , \tag{8.8}$$

$$c_t = c_{sea\_mile\_ton} \times m_{sea} + c_{land\_mile\_ton} \times m_{land} \; , \tag{8.9}$$

where

C_{init}	is the initial transportation cost,
c_{vd}	is the cost of value depreciation,
V_{cargo}	is the value of the cargo,
$\%V_{dp}$	is the value depreciation per day,
d	is the number of days to transport goods from source to destination,
c_t	is the transportation cost,
c_o	is the overhead cost,
$C_{sea\_mile\_ton}$	is the cost of transport by sea per mile-ton,
$C_{land\_mile\_ton}$	is the cost of transport by land per mile-ton,
m_{sea}	is the distance between two ports by sea, and
m_{land}	is the distance between two ports by land.

8.2.2.2 *System modeling*

The problem is formulated as a network optimization problem where the objective function is to maximize the total flow on the network links shown in Fig. 8.2, so that each node receives and sends its required demand to and from the rest of the network. The tonnage flow along the maritime routes is required to determine some of the resilience metrics. The network optimization problem is to maximize the tonnage flow between the ports. The optimization problem is given by Eqs. (8.10)–(8.14):

$$\text{Maximize } Total\_Tonnage \tag{8.10}$$

subject to the constraints

$$\sum_{j=1}^{n} x_{ij} = Tn\_in_i \ , \tag{8.11}$$

$$\sum_{i=1}^{n} x_{ij} = Tn\_out_j \ , \tag{8.12}$$

$$\sum_{i=1}^{n} x_{ij} \geq Tn_{ij} \ , \tag{8.13}$$

$$x_{ij} \geq 0 \ , \tag{8.14}$$

where

x_{ij} is the flow between two nodes i and j,

Tn_in_i is the tonnage into node i,

Tn_out_j is the tonnage out of node j, and

Tn_{ij} is the tonnage between node i and node j.

The approximation of the total tonnage per day is based on information on total cargo volume and container traffic provided by the American Association of Port Authorities (AAPA 2007). The shipping time is estimated using a systems dynamic model that calculates the average time it takes to process ships depending on the available port capacity. A reduction in the port capacity will prolong the time it takes to process the ships.

The time resilience assessment is carried out on a port-to-port basis that is based on the time it takes the ships to reach their destination. The systems dynamic model shown in Fig. 8.3 is used to estimate the travel time from Port A to Port B. Running the model requires knowledge of the number of ships per day going into Port B and the port's capacity. The two stocks in the model are *Ships at Port A Destined for Port B* and *Ships Waiting to Be Processed at Port B*. The model assumes that Port B can accept a certain number of ships per day from Port A, which is specified by the *Ships Processed by Port B per Day* variable, and no more ships are sent out of Port A if the *Maximum No. of Ships Allowed at Port B* parameter is exceeded, which will in turn increase the *Ships Stuck at Port A* parameter.

The *Total System Travel Time* parameter takes into account the *Travel time from Port A to Port B, Time waiting at Port B, and Ships Stuck at Port A* parameters. Hypothetical disruptions are introduced by reducing the *Port B capacity* parameter. A more accurate representation of the network is achievable by expanding the system dynamics model to include all the ports in the network model.

- **Disruption Scenarios**

When disruptions occur, the recovery procedures may last several days until the full operational capacity is restored. Figure 8.4 shows an example of a disruptive profile that lasts for three days. The initial

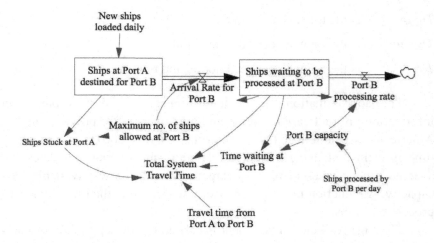

Fig. 8.3. Systems dynamics model for measuring total system travel time.

impact reduces the port capacity to 30 percent, while on the second and third days, 50 percent and 75 percent of the operating capacity is recovered respectively.

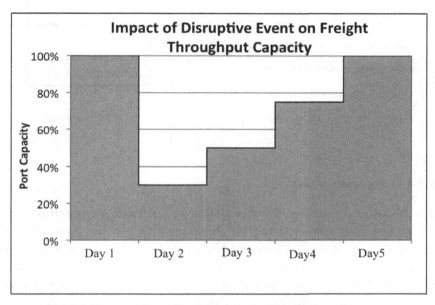

Fig. 8.4. Port capacity profile under the influence of a disruptive event.

8.2.3 *Resilience scheme identification*

Resilience schemes aim at improving the resilience of the system. In Chap. 4, several resilience schemes that reduce the vulnerability and increase the adaptive capacity of the system were suggested.

This case study evaluates the impact of Collaboration (Sec. 4.3.3) on the resilience metrics. Implementation of the Collaboration scheme entails Diversity (Sec. 4.2.3). The Collaboration scheme will be evaluated for ports that are linked by land where the transported tonnage may continue its journey by alternative transportation means such as trains and trucks. This scheme also requires Resource Allocation (Sec. 4.3.1) in order to make the necessary preparations such as the allocation of trucks, trains and personnel for transferring the goods. These three schemes are highlighted in Fig. 8.5.

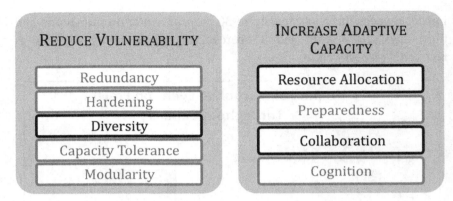

Fig. 8.5. Resilience schemes for MTS.

8.2.4 *Case study results*

The resilience evaluation for this system is performed on a port-to-port basis. The two ports selected for the evaluation are the ports of Los Angeles/Long Beach (LA/LB) and Shanghai. The resilience analysis was carried out on ships entering LA/LB. The optimization problem defined in Eqs. (8.10)–(8.14) was programmed and run using Microsoft Excel and Solver. The optimization problem relays information about the approximate tonnage flow along the maritime routes.

- **Critical Node and Link Identification**

The critical ports are those that have the most tonnage flow in and out of them. The network model shown in Fig. 8.2, along with Eqs. (8.10)–(8.14), was used to determine the most critical node in that network. For this particular network, the most critical port was identified to be the Port of Los Angeles/Long Beach followed by the Port of Singapore.

Singapore is one of the busiest ports in the world (AAPA 2007). The network model supports this fact, indicating that the route between Singapore and Hong Kong is the busiest in this network.

- **Resilience Analysis**

Tonnage resilience is determined by the tonnage the port is capable of processing following a disruptive event. According to the demand values, which were determined through the use of the network model shown in Fig. 8.2, the total tonnage received by LA/LB from the other ports in the network was calculated to be 325,000 tons daily. This is equivalent to approximately 21 ships, assuming that each ship carries 3,000 containers, with a maximum of five tons each.

Since LA/LB is already operating at 100 percent of its capacity, the relationship between the severity of the disruption and the resilience value is linear. The tonnage resilience of the disruptive event shown in Fig. 8.4 was calculated using Eqs. (8.2)–(8.4). The tonnage resilience over three days was measured to be 0.65, which indicates that the port operates at only 65 percent of its original capacity over that period. The impact of the disruptive event profile shown in Fig. 8.4 on the time resilience was evaluated using the systems dynamic model shown in Fig. 8.3. The model was programmed and simulated using Vensim PLE.

Equation (8.5) was used to calculate the time resilience based on the *Total System Travel Time* variable in the Vensim model. The introduction of the disruption profile described by Fig. 8.4 decreases the travel time resilience to 0.62. This means that it takes 38 percent more time to process the ships.

The final resilience metric is the cost resilience from a transportation perspective. Assuming that the average value of the goods carried by the ships is US$60 million, and the value of goods depreciates at a rate of 5 percent per day, the Vensim model shows that ships wait an average of three days before they are processed. This wait incurs a cost of US$9 million. If the initial transportation cost, including insurance and security, is US$49.5 million, the cost resilience, calculated from Eqs. (8.6)–(8.9), is 0.85. Thus, the disruption incurred transportation costs of 15 percent.

The results of the resilience analysis are summarized in Fig. 8.6.

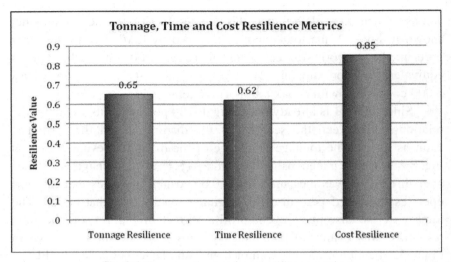

Fig. 8.6. Tonnage, time, and cost resilience metrics.

- **Resilience Scheme Identification**

The system's resilience can be enhanced through the implementation of resilience schemes that reduce the vulnerability of the system and increase its adaptive capacity. Rerouting the ships through other ports is one way of reducing the vulnerability. The adaptive capacity can be increased through collaborative efforts between ports, by receiving goods by sea and transporting them on through the use of parallel systems such as trains and trucks.

Since LA/LB is connected by land to Oakland, the Port of Oakland may have enough capacity to receive ships that would otherwise have remained at the source port. The cargo can then be transported from the Port of Oakland to LA/LB by train or truck. This scenario was simulated using a Vensim model that takes into account the time it takes to transport goods from Shanghai to Oakland by sea and then from Oakland to LA/LB by land. The results of the simulation showed that the travel time resilience increases from 0.62 to 0.70, which is an improvement of 8 percent. The assumption here is that only those ships that would have remained at the destination due to the disruption are rerouted to other ports.

The cost of shipping the goods to either LA/LB or Oakland is almost the same. With prior knowledge of the disruption, the additional costs of shipping to LA/LB will include shipping the containers by land from Oakland to LA/LB. Intermodal rail is a popular means of transporting containers by land since it is cheaper than trucks (McGregor 2006). It also consumes less fuel and does not create road congestion (Batchelor 2009).

Shipping the containers from Oakland to LA/LB costs 2.7 cents per mile-ton and would require an extra day to transport. Taking into account depreciation as a result of the delay, the cost of land transportation and the overhead costs, the cost resilience is calculated as 0.9. This figure indicates a 5 percent improvement on the previously calculated cost resilience value.

Figure 8.7 shows the impact of port collaboration on the system's resilience metrics.

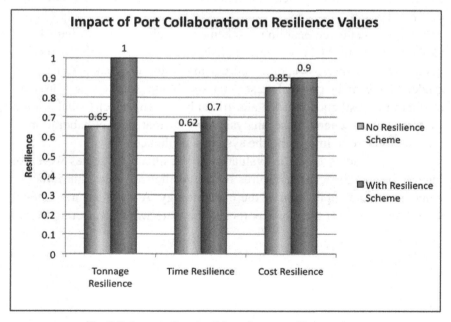

Fig. 8.7. Impact of port collaboration on resilience values.

8.3 Summary

The global waterways are the primary means of transporting goods. Hence, a disruption in the maritime transportation system directly influences the global economy. In addition, due to their geographic location, maritime ports are particularly vulnerable to both natural disasters and intentional attacks. It is crucial, therefore, to implement resilience in this infrastructure system in order to prepare it in the face of threats so that normal operation can be resumed with minimum losses.

In this chapter, the NIRA framework was applied to the maritime transportation infrastructure and several resilience metrics were proposed. The resilience metrics measure the impact of disruption on the performance measures of the system, which are the capacity of the ports to send and receive goods, the speed of delivery, and transportation cost. Based on these performance measures, the identified resilience metrics for this infrastructure system are tonnage resilience, time resilience and cost resilience.

One resilience-enabling scheme specified in Chap. 4 is Collaboration. In MTS systems, collaboration allows ports to receive goods by land through another port using trains or trucks. A network model of the main ports of East Asia and North America was used to evaluate the resilience metrics and to study the impact of Collaboration as a resilience scheme. The analysis showed that port collaboration is indeed effective in improving the system's resilience.

The examples used for evaluating the resilience schemes were not intended to obtain accurate figures for the resilience values, but rather to demonstrate the application of the methodology. A more accurate model would include all of the world ports and the waterways connecting them.

Chapter 9

Assessing the Resilience of Enterprise Systems — An ITS Case Study

The research so far has attempted to measure the resilience of physical networked infrastructure systems. In this chapter, the NIRA framework is applied to an enterprise system, in particular, the US National Intelligent Transportation System (ITS). Our resilience analysis is based around social network analysis.

Enterprise architectures define the structure of organizations and the linkages between the various components that make up the architecture. The National Intelligent Transportation System is represented by a physical architecture defining the components and a logical architecture defining how these components are linked to one another.

In social networks, the actors are the nodes in the network and the interactions between the actors are the network links. The logical architecture of enterprise systems can be thought of as a social network where the nodes are the processes and the links are the data flows between the processes.

In this chapter, the NIRA framework is applied to the elements that make up the emergency operations network in the National Intelligent Transportation System architecture.

9.1 Problem Statement

The physical layer of an infrastructure system would cease to function without the support of the organizational layer. In order to have a comprehensive resilience analysis of an infrastructure system, it is vital to measure and test resilience schemes at the enterprise level.

This chapter extends the application of the NIRA framework to the organizational architecture, where the nodes are the processes or activities that the organization undertakes, and the links are the data flows between the processes.

9.2 Overview of National ITS

The National ITS architecture contains detailed information about the functions required by the ITS, the entities that carry out these functions, and the information flows that connect the functions. A complete description of the architecture is defined by both physical and logical architectures (USDOT 2008).

9.2.1 *The physical architecture*

The physical architecture is made up of four main subsystems, categorized as follows:

- the institutions or enterprises that govern the operation of the infrastructure system,
- the physical components of the infrastructure system,
- the individuals using the system, and
- the devices that connect the users to other subsystems.

Centers, *Field*, *Travelers* and *Vehicles* represent these subsystems in the National ITS:

Centers: This subsystem contains ITS functions such as traffic management, emergency management, and maintenance and construction.

Field: This subsystem contains the physical elements of the infrastructure system, such as the equipment that enables traffic management operations, roadway safety measures, security monitoring, toll collection, etc.

Travelers: This subsystem provides users with services such as traffic information, transit stations and other fixed points along the route.

Vehicles: This subsystem includes the sensory and communication devices inside vehicles that support safe and efficient vehicle operation.

Road vehicles are categorized into basic vehicles, commercial vehicles, transit vehicles, maintenance and construction vehicles, and emergency vehicles.

The physical architecture of the National ITS is shown in Fig. 9.1.

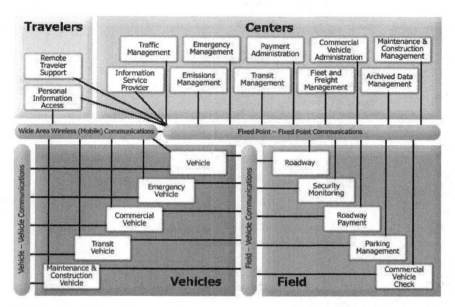

Fig. 9.1. Physical architecture of the National ITS. Source: *www.iteris.com/itsarch/ html/entity/paents.htm.*

9.2.2 *The logical architecture*

The logical architecture includes detailed information on the functions that were identified in the Centers subsystem of the physical architecture as well as the shared information flow between them. The functions in the logical architecture are known as *processes,* and the shared information between the functions are called *data flows.* The logical architecture is made up of several hierarchical levels, where each level is described by a data flow diagram (DFD). The first level is the context diagram that identifies the external components that interact with the National ITS. The second level is DFD0, which describes the interactions between the main processes. Figure 9.2 shows a high-level description of DFD0 for the logical architecture of the National ITS.

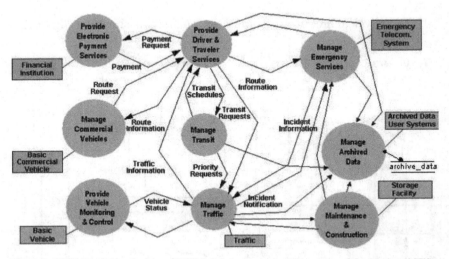

Fig. 9.2. High-level description of DFD0 for the logical architecture of the National ITS.
Source: *www.iteris.com/itsarch/html/menu/laindex.htm.*

9.3   Resilience Assessment of the National ITS Emergency Operations

9.3.1 *Boundary definition*

The first step of the framework is to define the analysis boundary. The boundaries specified by the NIRA framework are the spatial, operational and temporal boundaries.

9.3.1.1 *Spatial boundaries*

The spatial boundary defines the nodes and links that make up the network model. The NIRA framework is applied to assess resilience against disruptions of the processes involved in emergency operations. Emergency operations include entities that can sense a disruption in traffic or traffic operations, and entities that are involved in response and recovery procedures.

9.3.1.2 *Operational boundaries*

The operational boundaries are defined by the data flows between the processes. The National ITS logical architecture contains a compete list of data flows between all the entities in the architecture. Therefore, the specification of operational boundaries involves the extraction of the data flows relevant to the emergency operations from the logical architecture.

9.3.1.3 *Temporal boundaries*

The temporal bounaries are based on the assumption that it takes a certain amount of time for infromation to be transferred from one process to another over a particular data flow link. The network model will be used to assess the impact of disruptions on the time it takes the data to travel from the source to the destination node.

9.3.2 *Resilience assessment process*

9.3.2.1 *Resilience metric definition*

The NIRA framework proposes measuring resilience as the ratio between the value delivery of the system before a disruption, and after a disruption. The resilience is measured in terms of the impact of the disruption on the value delivery of the system. Disruptive events cause the value delivery to deteriorate, and the deterioration may either increase or decrease the magnitude of the value delivery of the system. The value delivery is represented by the performance measures of the network. Equation (9.1) shows the resilience metrics for both scenarios:

$$R(t) = \begin{cases} \dfrac{V_{after\_shock}}{V_{before\_shock}} & \text{for } \left| PM_{before\_shock} \right| > \left| PM_{after\_shock} \right|, \\[2ex] \dfrac{V_{before\_shock}}{V_{after\_shock}} & \text{for } \left| PM_{before\_shock} \right| < \left| PM_{after\_shock} \right|, \end{cases} \tag{9.1}$$

where V is the value delivery of the system and PM is the performance measure that defines the value delivery.

Several metrics have been defined for measuring the performance of social networks. The four most commonly used centrality measures are degree centrality, betweenness centrality, closeness centrality, and eigenvector centrality. An introduction to these different measures was given in Chap. 5.

Newman (2003) proposed using betweenness centrality as an indication of the network resilience. Betweenness centrality is a measure of how often a node lies in the shortest paths between other nodes in the network. Networks with a higher average node betweenness are less resilient, since one node lies in numerous paths.

We propose to use closeness centrality as a resilience measure. The closeness centrality metric determines how accessible one node is to the rest of the network. Using this metric, we are able to determine the amount of time it takes the flow to reach the node as well as to investigate the impact of reducing the capacity of the communication link. The degree centrality is utilized in the vulnerability analysis, where the critical nodes in the network are identified.

The following sections will elaborate on closeness centrality, how it is obtained and how the resilience of this metric can be measured.

- **Closeness Centrality Resilience**

The closeness centrality metric was defined by Freeman (1979) as the mean geodesic distance between a node and all other nodes. The geodesic distance is the shortest path between two nodes where a path is the sum of links connecting two nodes. Borgatti (2005) defines closeness in the context of flow as the expected time until the arrival of something flowing through the network.

Disruptions may partially or fully sever the communication links between the nodes, and hence it takes more time for the flow to reach a node that has a low closeness score. On the other hand, nodes with high closeness scores tend to receive flows sooner. It is assumed that the flow will take the shortest path between any two nodes. Assuming that the time it takes for information to travel between node i and node j is t, and that the weight of the link is w, we propose that the closeness centrality of node v can be measured as shown in Eq. (9.2).

$$C_c(v) = \frac{\sum_{\substack{s \in V \\ s \neq v}}^{n} d_G(v,s) \cdot wt}{n-1} , \qquad (9.2)$$

where

d_G	is the geodesic distance between node i and node j,
v	are the nodes in the network,
t	is the time it takes for information to flow from node i to node j,
w	is the number time units, and
n	is the number of nodes in the network.

Equation (9.2) assumes that the time it takes for the information to flow over the link is determined by its weight w. The weight of the link w determines the increase in time as a result of a disruption; increasing the weight increases the closeness centrality score.

Using Eq. (9.1), the closeness centrality resilience R_{cc} is given by:

$$R_{cc} = \frac{C_c(v)_{before\_shock}}{C_c(v)_{after\_shock}} , \qquad (9.3)$$

where

$$C_c(v)_{before\_shock} = \frac{\sum_{\substack{s \in V \\ s \neq v}}^{n} d_G(v,s) \cdot wt}{n-1} \qquad (9.4)$$

and

$$C_c(v)_{after\_shock} = \frac{\sum_{\substack{s \in V \\ s \neq v}}^{n} d_G(v,s) \cdot wt_{after\_shock}}{n-1} . \qquad (9.5)$$

9.3.2.2 *System modeling*

The system model is based on the logical architecture of the National ITS, which is made up of several hierarchical levels of DFDs. Level 0 of the architecture is the context diagram showing the inputs and outputs of the ITS and the interactions with entities external to the system. The first level of the logical architecture (DFD0) shows the highest level of the system's structure, which includes the main processes and the interactions between them. The system model used for the analysis is based on DFD0 (for the logical architcture), which is composed of several processes that relate to different functions of the physical entities in the ITS architecture.

The resilience assessment is based on the reaction of the system to emergency situations. The network used for the analysis is shown in Fig. 9.3. It is extracted from the logical architecture by including the processes that are involved in reacting to emergencies, which include the emergency information flow between the processes.

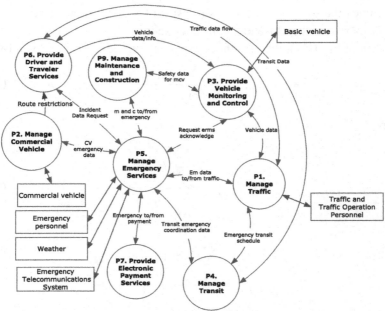

Fig. 9.3. Emergency interactions extracted from the National ITS logical architecture.

The processes are linked to the sources that can potentially cause and detect disruptions on the road, such as basic vehicles, commercial vehicles and traffic. The data flows transfer the information that triggers the correct response from the different processes in order to carry out the emergency and recovery operations.

• **Critical Link Identification**

The critical nodes in the network are those that require special attention when addressing the network's resilience. The social network analysis measures such as degree centrality, eigenvector centrality and betweenness centrality are used to determine those links.

The degree centrality of a node was introduced by Freeman (1979), who defined it as the number of direct links that are connected to the node. Borgatti defined it as the number of paths of length one that emanate from a node (Borgatti 2005). A disruption that causes the node with the highest degree to collapse will result in the maximum number of severed links. A standardized value of the degree centrality of a node is calculated by summing up the links connected to that node and dividing by the sum of the rest of the nodes in the network, as given by Eq. (9.6):

$$C_D(v)_{after\_shock} = \frac{\sum_{i=1}^{n} a(v,s)}{n-1} \quad \text{for } s \in V \;, \tag{9.6}$$

where

a is a link connected to node v,
V are the nodes in the network,
k is the number of nodes connected to node v, and
n is the number of nodes in the network.

Another measure that is frequently used to determine the most important nodes in the network is the eigenvector centrality. A more sophisticated version of degree centrality, the eigenvector centrality metric takes into account the type of direct link that is connected to a node. A higher node eigenvector value means that the node is connected to other "more important" nodes in the network (Newman 2008). However, the eigenvector centrality can only be applied to symmetric networks.

- **Disruption Scenarios**

The resilience of the network is assessed by introducing hypothetical disruptions into the network. Under normal operating conditions, the resilience value is one. This value may be reduced to zero depending on the severity of the disruption.

Disruptions may decrease the operating capacity of a link or even sever a link completely. Reducing the number of links will consequently increase the workload in the remaining links. As a result, the time it takes for the data flow to be sent or received increases. Several studies, such as that by Andre (2001), have tried to establish a relationship between the increase in workload and time-to-task completion. Here, we define the relationship between the increase in workload and the time-to-task completion by:

$$t_{after\_shock} = \lambda t , \tag{9.7}$$

where λ is the coefficient that reflects the increase in time as a result of the increase in workload, and t is the information flow time. The closeness centrality resilience is measured by substituting into Eq. (9.3) the values of t and t_{after_shock} determined by Eq. (9.7).

9.3.3 *Resilience scheme selection*

9.3.3.1 *Resilience scheme identification*

Resilience-enabling schemes allow the system to recover and resume normal functionality in the shortest time. These schemes are also designed to ensure that the system is able to deliver the required performance in the face of threats.

Chapter 4 identified several schemes that improve the resilience of systems. These schemes are shown in Fig. 9.4. The resilience of an ITS network is improved by reducing the time it takes for the data to flow from one node to another. The two identified resilience-enabling schemes that are particularly useful for performing this task are Resource Allocation (Sec. 4.3.1) and Collaboration (Sec. 4.3.3). Resource Allocation entails reorganizing resources so that the link capacities may be utilized for rerouting purposes in addition to their normal workload.

Collaboration between the various parties involved in the different processes facilitates the establishment of direct links between all the nodes in order to compensate for disrupted links.

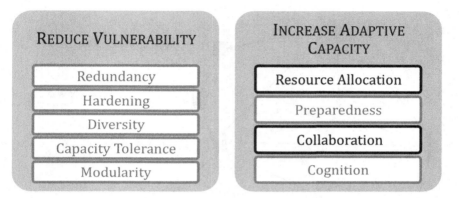

Fig. 9.4. Resilience schemes for ITS emergency operations.

9.3.3.2 *Resilience scheme evaluation*

The suitability of the scheme will depend on factors such as feasibility and cost. A better understanding of which is the most beneficial scheme to deploy is achieved through the application of a structured decision analysis process that enables the decision makers to choose between the alternatives under uncertainty.

A disruption will increase the time it takes the data flow to reach the node it is intended for. The delay will incur financial losses for the network itself as well as other interdependent networks such as the transportation infrastructure. As the resilience schemes are deployed for the duration of the disruptive event, consideration must be given to the time aspect.

9.3.4 *Case study results*

The program UCINET was used to create the network model and to perform the social network analysis. The network is made up of eight nodes corresponding to eight of the processes in DFD0 for the logical architecture. The network links represent the information flow between the nodes. This is a directed network and is asymmetric. Figure 9.5 shows the network used for the analysis.

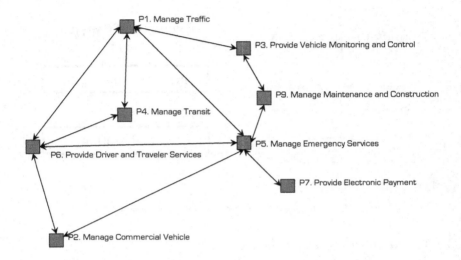

Fig. 9.5. Social network of emergency operations.

• Critical Node Identification

The degree centrality score was used to determine the most critical node in the network. The node with the highest degree centrality score has the largest number of direct links, and the impact of a disruption is maximized if that particular node is affected.

Figure 9.6 shows the degree centrality scores of all the nodes in the network. Since the network is focused on emergency operations, node P5 "Manage Emergency Services" has, as expected, the highest possible score, and this is therefore the most critical node. The degree centrality scores of the rest of the network nodes are between 14.3 and 57.1, a range of values that is much lower than the score of node P5. This is an indication that the network is centralized around P5. Hence, disruptions at this node would almost disintegrate the network.

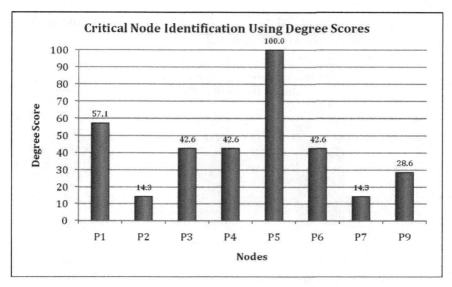

Fig. 9.6. Critical node identification using degree scores.

• **Closeness Centrality Resilience Assessment**

The sources of disruptions vary in nature and severity. Sources of disruption that result in traffic congestions and loss of time and money are the vehicles on the road (such as basic vehicles and commercial vehicles) and increases in traffic volume. The emergency information obtained from these three sources is linked to the ITS network by the processes P1, P2 and P3, as shown in Fig. 9.5. Our vulnerability analysis shows that the most critical node in the network is node P5, so the disruption scenarios are introduced into the links that connect node P5 to nodes P1, P2 and P3. Disruptions are introduced by deleting network links.

Deleting the link between P1 and P5 increases the time it takes to transfer the information between P1 and P5, since the information has to travel over a longer path. A delay due to increasing workload volumes is also incurred. The delay was measured by assuming a value of 1.1 for λ in Eq. (9.7). This value was chosen to add a small increase in the data transfer time. Using Eqs. (9.3)–(9.5), the closeness resilience metrics for

P1 and P5 were calculated to be 0.699 and 0.795, respectively. The resilience values are shown in Figure 9.7.

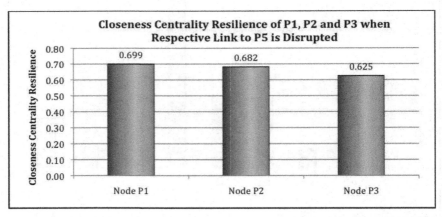

Fig. 9.7. Closeness centrality resilience values for nodes P1, P2, P3 when links P1–P5, P2–P5, P3–P5 are disrupted.

- **Resilience Scheme**

Improving the resilience value is achievable through the implementation of resilience schemes. One of the resilience schemes considered is Resource Allocation, where the basic structure of the network remains unchanged. In this case, routing the information over the existing nodes entails reducing the time it takes to transfer the information over the shortest path.

In order to maintain a resilience value of one, the time it takes to transfer the information over the shortest path must be no longer than $0.8t$, which is 20 percent faster than the normal rate. The graphs in Fig. 9.8 show the closeness centrality resilience for different λ values. The improvement in the values of the resilience metric is around 20 percent for each of P1, P2 and P3 when λ is set to 0.8. Node P5 exhibits an extremely resilient behavior for values of λ less than 0.85, with resilience values exceeding unity.

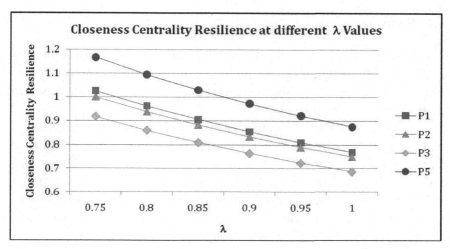

Fig. 9.8. Closeness centrality resilience for different λ values.

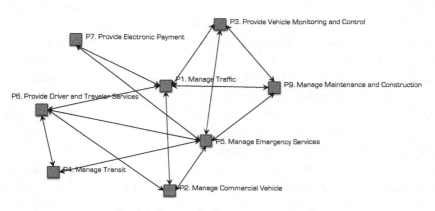

Fig. 9.9. Reorganized emergency network.

The other proposed resilience scheme is Collaboration, which entails a reorganization of the network through the addition of extra links between the disrupted node and the rest of the nodes that are not directly connected. Figure 9.9 shows a reorganized network when the link between P1 and P5 is disrupted and new direct links are established to compensate for the disrupted link.

9.4 Summary

The logical and physical architectures of enterprise systems define the structure of the enterprise; that is, the main functions of the enterprise, how the functions work together, as well as the external entities that interact with the enterprise system.

In this case study, we demonstrated how enterprise architectures can be viewed as networked infrastructure systems using established social network analysis techniques. In social networks, the nodes represent the actors and the links represent the information flow between the actors. Similar logic can be applied to enterprise architectures, where the nodes represent the main functions or processes of the enterprise, and the links represent how the functions interact with one another.

The NIRA framework proposes a methodology for measuring the resilience of a networked infrastructure system in which resilience is measured as the impact of disruptions on the system's performance measures. The framework was applied to the emergency operations network of the National ITS, which was modeled as a social network.

There are several measures for quantifying social networks, including degree centrality and closeness centrality. For our purposes, the closeness centrality metric was used for measuring the resilience, since it is an indication of how well the information flows through the network. In addition to the traditional definition of closeness centrality, the link time factor λt was introduced to represent the amount of time it takes for information to flow from one node to another. The degree centrality metric measures how well a node is connected. This metric was used to identify the most critical nodes in the network that would cause the maximum network damage when disrupted.

Applying this methodology to measure enterprise resilience requires well-defined physical and logical architectures of the enterprise system. Enterprise networks are often complex and have several processes running in parallel, and a disruption may impact only some of the processes. A resilience analysis following a disruption requires the extraction of the elements impacted by the disruption into a sub-network. Thus, several sub-networks are required to assess the resilience against different sources of disruptions.

Chapter 10

Conclusion

Infrastructure resilience received considerable attention after the September 11 attacks in 2001. Since then, the resilience of infrastructure systems has come under renewed scrutiny following several other severe disruptive events, including the 2004 Indian Ocean tsunami and its impact on the maritime infrastructure, and the Icelandic ash cloud in 2010 and the implications for the air transportation infrastructure.

The main contributions of this book are threefold: (i) an in-depth study of the concept of resilience and its relationship to various system properties ("ilities" such as flexibility); (ii) the presented Networked Infrastructure Resilience Assessment (NIRA) framework, which proposes step-by-step procedures to measure the resilience of networked infrastructures; and (iii) the suggested sets of resilience metrics based on a system's key performance measures. The book began with an overview of what resilience means for infrastructure systems, how it relates to other known system properties and several schemes that enhance infrastructure resilience.

The following sections of this chapter present a chapter-by-chapter summary of the book, an assessment of the validity of the research hypothesis, a summary of the contributions and limitations of the research, and an outline of the directions for future work.

10.1 Book Summary

Chapter 1 set out the framework of the book. The chapter began by highlighting the interest of the federal government and various stakeholders in implementing resilience in infrastructure systems. This was followed by a brief description of resilience, what the concept means for infrastructure systems, and why there is a need to implement resilience in those systems. In addition, our hypothesis for measuring networked infrastructure resilience was presented. The hypothesis implied that the resilience of an infrastructure system can be measured by assessing the impact of disruptions on the key performance measures of the system, and that disruptions manifest themselves in the form of capacity reductions in the network's links and nodes.

The literature review in Chap. 2 looked at the various definitions of resilience found in research contributions to date, as well as at the sources of disruptions and catastrophic events. Although the study of resilience in engineering systems is fairly new, researchers have put forward several methodologies for its characterization. Several resilience metrics have also been proposed for the different service infrastructure systems. Our literature review revealed that an effective way of enhancing a system's resilience is by reducing its vulnerability, thereby reducing the susceptibility of the system to disruptions and increasing its adaptive capacity. This allows the system to resume normal or near-normal operation in the shortest time possible. Throughout the book, the concept of reducing the vulnerability and increasing the adaptive capacity was used as the basis for achieving resilience in infrastructure systems. Chapter 2 also looked into how resilience in organizations can be achieved, given that the organizational layer is a critical component of infrastructure systems.

Chapter 3 presented a comparative study between resilience and other well-known system properties; namely reliability, robustness, flexibility and agility. These terms often appear together and in some cases are used interchangeably. This chapter provided a definition of each of these properties and an overview of some of the metrics used in their measurement. The analysis showed that the major similarities and differences are in what the system is prepared against (type of failure), the causes of the failure (uncertainty), and how the system reacts to overcome the failure (level of adaptability).

Reliability deals with the response of the system to internal failures. Robustness, flexibility and agility deal with the system's response to both internal and external failures. Resilience deals with the response of the system to severe internal and external disruptions. Reliability deals with "known unknowns" (uncertainty that can be analyzed and identified), while robustness, flexibility, agility and resilience are concerned with "unknown unknowns." Robust and reliable systems do not adapt to disruptions by changing their basic structure; flexible, agile and resilient systems, on the other hand, have the ability to reconfigure in order to adapt to the new circumstances created by disruptions. Figure 10.1 shows the differences between reliability, robustness, flexibility, agility and resilience (also referred to as R^2FAR) in terms of types of failures, uncertainty and adaptability.

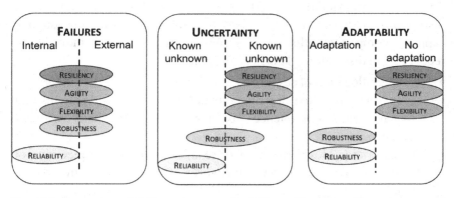

Fig. 10.1. Comparing reliability, robustness, flexibility, agility and resilience in terms of failures, uncertainty and adaptability.

Chapter 4 looked at the different schemes that enable systems to be more resilient in the face of disruptions. The schemes are derived based on the elements of resilience; that is, the vulnerability and adaptive capacity. Reducing the vulnerability of a system reduces its susceptibility to disruptions, while the adaptive capacity component allows the system to resume functionality after the occurrence of a disruptive event. Several schemes that promote these two elements of resilience were suggested; these schemes are shown in Fig. 10.2.

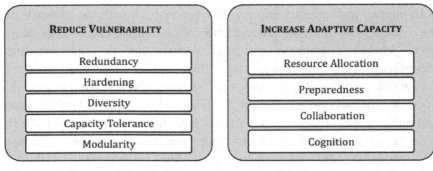

Fig. 10.2. Resilience enablers for reducing vulnerability and increasing adaptive capacity.

Schemes such as Redundancy, Hardening, Diversity, Capacity Tolerance and Modularity reduce the susceptibility of systems to disruptions and hence make them less vulnerable. Increasing the adaptive capacity component allows the system to react quickly in order to recover from disruptions. This is achievable by:

- proper allocation of resources,
- preparing the system for disruptions by implementing policies that manage the consequences of threats and facilitate recovery procedures,
- collaboration in order to achieve seamless sending and receiving of information across all the subnetworks of the infrastructure system, and
- making the infrastructure system more cognitive; that is, the ability to perceive the changes that occur in it, select a course of action to deal with the current situation, and keep track of the system's behavior for the implemented course of action for future reference.

Chapter 5 introduced our proposed Networked Infrastructure Resilience Assessment (NIRA) framework, the core contribution of the book. The framework is made up of six steps grouped into the following three stages: boundary definition, the resilience assessment process, and resilience scheme identification. The NIRA framework aids decision makers in assessing the resilience of networked infrastructure systems and in evaluating the benefits of the appropriate resilience schemes. A system's resilience can be measured by assessing the impact of disruptions on the value delivery of the system by taking a ratio of the value delivery before and after the occurrence of a disruptive event. The chapter elaborated on each of the steps of the framework and proposed several methodologies for modeling networked infrastructure systems. The NIRA framework is shown in Fig. 10.3.

Chapters 6 to 9 presented a series of case studies that illustrate the application of the NIRA framework to four different types of infrastructure systems. In Chap. 6, the NIRA framework was applied to the telecommunications infrastructure, and the resilience of the global trans-oceanic submarine cable system was assessed. The value delivery of the system was identified as the amount of data transferred across the telecommunications cables in gigabits per second. The physical system was modeled as a network, and a network optimization formula was used to estimate the impact of capacity reduction of the links on the data transferred in the cables. The deployment of the capacity tolerance scheme to reroute the information over residual network capacities improved the resilience value. The successful implementation of this scheme entails the deployment of the resource allocation scheme, which improves the adaptive capacity. Proper resource allocation allows for quick adjustments of system resources such as equipment and staff in order to accommodate the changes.

Chapter 7 presented two distinct cases studies, both related to transportation infrastructure. The road network is a particularly important component of transportation infrastructure, since roads are the primary means of transport for passengers traveling from one city to another and for the movement of goods between cities and towns.

The first case study was to assess the resilience of the road network connecting Boston with New York City. The identified performance measures that form the basis of the resilience assessments were travel time, environmental impact and transportation cost. The case study looked at the impact of reducing the road capacities on the network resilience. The Diversity resilience-enabling scheme entails the use of other available transportation modes such as air and rail. Using these travel options, mode choice analysis was conducted in order to investigate the impact of disruption on air and rail travel when the road network is congested.

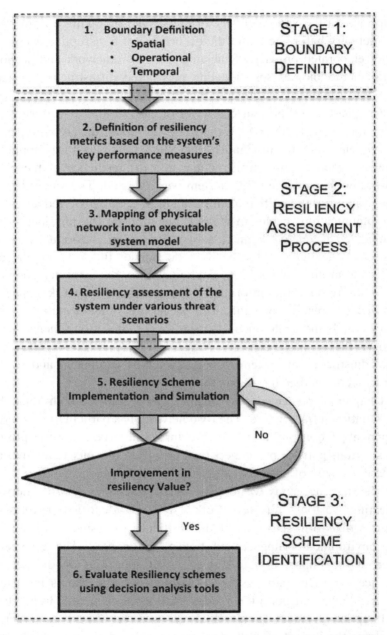

Fig. 10.3. The Networked Infrastructure Resilience Assessment (NIRA) framework.

The second case study looked at Manhattan's points of entry: the bridges and tunnels that are the primary access points into the island. The case study looked at the node-to-node resilience of the tunnels and bridges that connect Manhattan. Here again, disruptions were introduced by reducing the capacity of the tunnels and bridges. The case study illustrated the use of decision analysis in conjunction with cash flow theory to determine appropriate resilience schemes such as the use of ferries to transport passengers in cases of severe disruptions.

Chapter 8 assessed the resilience of maritime transportation systems (MTSs). Here, the network model represented the principal ports on both sides of the Pacific; the main ports in East Asia and North America. The identified value deliveries were tonnage, transportation time, and cost, since these are the most critical parameters for stakeholders. The disruption profile introduced mimicked the typical behavior of disruptions at ports over several days. It was shown that the most effective scheme for improving the resilience of the system in the face of disruptive events was collaboration between ports connected by land; allowing goods to make their way to the destination through alternative ports and then overland. Proper resource allocation was shown to be a key factor for ensuring the success of collaboration.

Chapter 9 presented a case study that falls outside of the realm of physical infrastructure systems. The purpose of this case study was to illustrate the application of the NIRA framework to non-physical networks such as those of enterprises or organizational systems. The NIRA framework was applied to the emergency operations network of the National Intelligent Transportation System (ITS). Extracted from the logical architecture of the ITS, the network was analyzed using known social network analysis tools. The proposed resilience metric was the closeness centrality metric, which represents the shortest distance between any two nodes. Resilience analysis of such networks requires well-defined physical and logical architectures of the enterprise systems under consideration.

10.2 Research Validation

The hypothesis of this research was that the resilience of the networked infrastructure system can be measured by assessing the impact of disruptions on the key performance measures of the system by introducing disruptions in the form of link/node capacity reductions.

The application of the NIRA framework was demonstrated in five systems that represent four different types of infrastructure systems. The integrity of the mathematical models developed to represent the infrastructure systems was validated through the following well-known research validation measures: construct validity, content validity, internal validity, external validity, criterion validity, and face validity (statistics.com 2004). The following sections describe how the case studies used to test our research hypothesis were evaluated using each of these validation measures.

10.2.1 *Construct validity*

Construct validity refers to the realistic representation of the system, that is, whether the mathematical models provide accurate data about the operation of the infrastructure systems presented in the case studies. In order to test the hypothesis, the models were required to replicate the data flow between the network nodes. The type of model depends on the type of operations in the infrastructure system.

In the Internet and transportation case studies, the models were set up using network flow theory. The optimization model included the objective functions and constraints that were formulated to obtain the network flows through which the system's performance measures (value deliveries) could be measured. A system dynamics model was constructed to determine the behavior of the system with time, such as in the MTS case study. The final case study applied the NIRA framework on an organizational network where the information flow was represented using social network analysis tools. The models were run under various input parameters and operating conditions to test for the consistency of the results.

10.2.2 *Content validity*

Content validity refers to the data used for conducting the analysis and how the models are used to obtain the measurements. The data used to set up the case study parameters were based on realistic capacity and demand data provided by the infrastructure managers, which are accessible to the general public. The NIRA framework first specifies the boundaries of the system; the boundary specification determines the scope of the analysis and the type of operation that determines the performance measures of the system. It was not possible to test for different data sets due to the unavailability of more data sets.

10.2.3 *Internal validity*

Internal validity refers to the relationship between the variables in the system model. The proposed resilience metric is based on the performance measure of the system. The performance measures of physical infrastructure systems are quantifiable values, thus yielding a resilience value that reflects the impact of disruptions on the system.

10.2.4 *External validity*

The external validity of the hypothesis is validated if the results obtained from one sample can be generalized to another set of samples. The hypothesis implied that disruptions could be modeled by reducing the capacity of the network links and/or nodes, which would consequently have an impact on the performance measures of the system. Although the nature of the sources of disruptions varied, their ultimate effect on the network is that the capacities of the network link and/or nodes were reduced. The severity of the disruptive event was modeled in terms of reducing the capacity of the network nodes and/or links. The NIRA framework was applied to five different case studies representing four different types of infrastructure systems. In each of the case studies, the simulation of the system model showed that disruptions in the form of a reduction in the capacity of the links and/or nodes worsened the values of the performance measures.

10.2.5 *Criterion validity*

Criterion validity compares results against a set of "gold standards"[1], thus emphasizing the credibility of the results. In order to test for criterion validity, the network models would have to be constructed using different approaches, such as modeling the same system using equation-based as well as agent-based modeling techniques. Although this type of validation is beyond the scope of this book, the direction of future studies is to apply different types of modeling techniques to a single system. For the presented case studies, criterion validity is tested by closely examining the relationships between the variables so that the results are within an acceptable range.

10.2.6 *Face validity*

Face validity depends on the judgment of the observer. It is tested for in terms of how the results appear to that observer. As such, face validity is tested by closely examining the results. Additionally, the results of the presented case studies have been submitted to and accepted by reputable scientific journals and peer-reviewed conferences.

The expert opinions of infrastructure managers also indicated that the NIRA framework is indeed a valid approach for assessing the resilience of infrastructure systems.

10.3 Research Contributions

This book presents a number of research contributions. These include literature synthesis, and conceptual, methodological and empirical contributions which are elaborated on in the following sections.

---

[1] *Gold standards* are results obtained by a well-established instrument or by direct measurement.

10.3.1 *Literature synthesis contribution (Chap. 2)*

The literature review provided in this book explored the concept of resilience in engineering systems as well as its appearance in other disciplines such as ecology, psychology and material science. Resilience was discussed in terms of the various definitions found in the literature, the methodologies that have been proposed to characterize resilience, and the metrics that have been put forward by researchers to measure the resilience of specific service infrastructure systems. The literature review also identified the key factors that contribute to organizational resilience.

10.3.2 *Conceptual contribution (Chaps. 3 and 4)*

Discourse on resilience often leads to discussions about reliability, robustness, flexibility and agility. This book clarified the similarities and differences between these concepts and what they mean for infrastructure systems. In addition to providing definitions and overviews of several metrics for measuring each of the attributes, these different system properties were compared with one another and with resilience. The major differences between reliability, robustness, flexibility, agility and resilience were found to be the source of disruptions a system is prepared for, the type of uncertainty that causes the disruptions, and the way the system reacts to the disruptions.

This book presented several resilience-enabling schemes, which were organized into two categories. The first category comprised schemes that reduce system vulnerability, thereby making the system less susceptible to disruptions. The second included schemes that increase a system's adaptive capacity, which allows that system to maintain functionality in the face of disruptions.

10.3.3 *Methodological contributions (Chap. 5)*

Currently, the majority of infrastructure stakeholders lack a tool for measuring the value of resilience in their infrastructure systems. Although researchers have proposed several metrics by which the resilience of specific systems can be assessed, as well as different ways for promoting resilience, there is no coherent resilience framework that can be applied to networked infrastructure systems in general.

The research outlined in this book aimed to fill this gap by presenting a single framework that enables stakeholders to measure the resilience of their respective infrastructure systems in a systemic manner, and to choose between different resilience-enabling schemes that improve the resilience of their infrastructure systems.

10.3.4 *Empirical contribution (Chaps. 6–9)*

The NIRA framework was applied to five case studies representing four different infrastructure systems: telecommunications networks, road transportation networks, maritime transportation networks, and enterprise systems. The case studies identified the key performance measures of each infrastructure system and how these performance measures can be used to assess the resilience of the system. For each of the case studies, the system boundaries were identified, the node-to-node and/or network resilience metric(s) were assessed, and the impact of introducing resilience schemes on the resilience values was evaluated. In addition, the case study considering Manhattan's entry-points road network demonstrated the application of decision trees and cash flow theory for evaluating resilience schemes.

10.4 Research Limitations

The proposed NIRA framework is intended for systems that are network-based. Most physical infrastructure systems can be represented as a network. Critical infrastructure systems such as health care systems and financial systems may require a different type of resilience assessment methodology.

Conducting an accurate resilience assessment requires accurate, up-to-date data. The data used for our case studies were obtained from sources that are available to the general public. However, in some cases, estimates had to be made in order to make up for a lack of data. Thus, the case studies aim to demonstrate the assessment process rather than present accurate resilience values for the infrastructure systems under consideration.

Another limitation of the NIRA framework is that it does not address the issue of interoperability between infrastructure systems due to cascading failures. The scope of the NIRA framework does not extend to assessing the impact of failures that propagate across infrastructure systems.

The resilience assessments obtained through the application of the NIRA framework do not account for human behavior nor the underlying confounding organizational issues.

10.4.1 *Interoperability issue*

The introductory chapter of this book stressed the importance of implementing resilience due to the interdependencies that exist between infrastructure systems. Therefore, given that infrastructure systems by their very nature do not exist in isolation, it is important to address disruptions that may affect more than one infrastructure system. Assessing the impact of disruptions that result from failures in parallel infrastructure systems provides more accurate resilience values.

In order to overcome this shortcoming of the NIRA framework, future studies will focus on studying the interactions between systems and how failures may propagate from one system to another.

10.4.2 *System modeling approaches*

The research detailed in this book used network optimization techniques, equation-based models and social network analysis. Future research will use agent-based modeling to model the interactions between the various elements of infrastructure systems.

10.4.3 *Application of NIRA framework to other types of systems*

Critical infrastructure systems have four dimensions, as shown in Fig. 10.4: physical, organizational, social and economic.

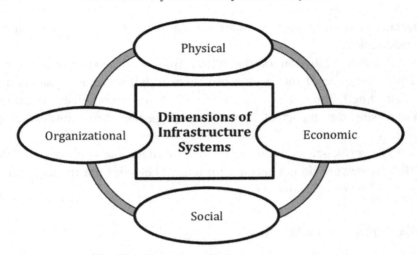

Fig. 10.4. Dimensions of infrastructure systems.

In this work, the framework was applied to the physical and organizational dimensions of infrastructure systems. The same assessment process can also be applied to the social and economic aspects, which are not physically networked systems, by identifying the important parameters of those infrastructure dimensions. Future studies will extend the scope to other types of systems that can be modeled as networks, such as supply chains.

10.5 Final Word

Infrastructure resilience is a relatively new field that is gaining increasing importance for governments and other stakeholders. This book has attempted to shed more light on this growing research area by proposing a methodology for measuring the resilience of networked infrastructure systems using a systems-based approach. The methodology put forward in this book does not provide solutions to every issue relating to resilience, but it is an important step towards understanding and quantifying resilience with a view to maintaining the performance, reliability and security of current infrastructure systems.

References

AAPA, (2007) *World Port Rankings 2007*, (American Association of Port Authorities).

Ahuja, R.K., Magnanti, T.L. and B., O.a.J., (1993). *Network Flows: Theory, Algorithms, and Applications*, (New Jersey, Prentice Hall).

Akçelik, R., (1991). Travel Time Functions for Transport Planning Purposes: Davidson's Function, its Time-Dependent Form and an Alternative Travel Time Function, *Australian Road Research*, **21** (3), pp. 49–59.

Amin, S.M. and Horowitz, B.M., (2008). Toward Agile and Resilient Large-Scale Systems: Adaptive Robust National/International Infrastructures, *Global Journal of Flexible Systems Management*, **9** (1).

Anderson, R.J., (2001). Natural Gas Infrastructure Reliability'. Strategic Center for Natural Gas.
URL: http://wpweb2.tepper.cmu.edu/ceic/presentations/Anderson.pdf

Andersson, E., (2006). Urban Landscapes and Sustainable Cities, *Ecology and Society*, **11** (1), p.34.

Andre, (2001) *Theoretical workload performance plot as a function of time*, (SkyBrary).
URL: http://www.skybrary.aero/index.php/Workload_(OGHFA_BN)

Andrews, J.D. and Ridley, L.M., (2002). Application of the cause-consequence diagram method to static systems, *Reliability Engineering and System Safety*, **75** (1), pp. 47–58.

AP, (2008). Third Internet Cable Cut in Middle East. *Fox News*.

Astaneh-Asla, A., (2008). Progressive collapse of steel truss bridges, the case of I-35W collapse, *Pros, 7th Int. Conf. on Steel Bridges*. Guimarães, Portugal.

Attoh-Okine, N., Cooper, A.T. and Mensah, S.A., (2009). Formulation of Resilience Index of Urban Infrastructure Using Belief Functions, *IEEE Systems Journal*, **3** (2), pp. 147–153.

Baker, J.W., Schubert, M. and Faber, M.H., (2008). On the assessment of robustness, *Science Direct – Structural Safety*, 30, pp. 253–267.

Batchelor, S., (2009). Shipping Freight Intermodal vs Traditional Truckload, SCexecutive, The Global Knowledge Network for Supply Chain Professionals.

Bell, M.A., (2002) *The Five Principles of Organizational Resilience* (Gartner).
URL: http://www.gartner.com/DisplayDocument?doc_cd=103658

Besemer, S., (2010) *Missouri SEMA Earthquake Program*.
URL: http://sema.dps.mo.gov/EQ.htm

Boehm, B. and Turner, R., (2004) *Balancing Agility and Discipline*: *A Guide for the Perplexed,* (Addison–Wesley Longman Publishing Co. Inc., Boston MA).

Borgatti, S.P., (2005). Centrality and network flow, *Social Networks*, **27**, pp. 55–71.

Borgatti, S.P., (2009). On Identifying Key Players In the Context of Network Flows.

Bottani, E., (2006). A fuzzy QFD approach to achieve agility, *International Journal of Production Economics*, **119** (2), pp. 380–391.

Brown, C.P., (2009). Climate change and Ontario forests: Prospects for building institutional adaptive capacity, *Mitigation and Adaptation Strategies for Global Change*, **14** (6), pp. 513–536.

Brown, T., (2006). Multiple Modeling Approaches and Insights for Critical Infrastructure Protection, National Infrastructure Simulation and Analysis Center.

Bruneau, M., Chang, S.E., Eguchi, R.T., Lee, G.C., O'Rourke, T.D., Reinhorn, A.M., Shinozuka, M., Tierney, K., Wallace, W.A. and vonWinterfeldt, D., (2003). A framework to quantitatively assess and enhance the seismic resilience of communities, *Earthquake Spectra*, **19** (4), pp. 733–752.

Bruneau, M. and Reinhorn, A., (2007). Exploring the Concept of Seismic Resilience for Acute Care Facilities, *Earthquake Spectra*, **23** (1), pp. 41–62.

Calabretta, R., (2009). *The Modularity Home Page*. URL: http://laral.istc.cnr.it/rcalabretta/modularity.html

Carpenter, S. and Brock, W., (2008). Adaptive Capacity and Traps, *Ecology and Society*, **13** (2), p. 40.

Chang, S.E. and Chamberlain, C., (2005). Assessing the role of lifeline systems in community disaster resilience, *Research Progress and Accomplishments 2003–2004*.

Clancy, T.P., (2009). The Maritime Transportation Security Act of 2002, *The CIP Report, Centre for Infrastructure Protection*, **7** (10).

Cohen, R., Erez, K., ben-Avraham, D. and Havlin, S., (2001). Breakdown of the internet under intentional attack, *Phy Rev Lett*, **86** (16), pp. 3682–3685.

Dalizell, E. and McManus, S., (2004). Resilience, Vulnerability, and Adaptive Capacity: Implications for System Performance, *International Forum on Engineering Decision Making*. Stoos, Switzerland.

DEMA, (2005) *DEMA's Approach to Risk and Vulnerability Analysis for Civil Contingency Planning*.
URL:http://www.brs.dk/folder/nationalsaarbarhedsrapport2005/Backgro und_paper_on_DEMAs_approach_to_risk_and_vulnerability_analysis. pdf

DoD, (1970). *Definitions of terms from reliability and maintainability,*. (Department of Defense, Washington, USA).

Dolev, D., Jamin, S., Mokryn, O. and Shavitt, Y., (2006). Internet resilience to attacks and failures under BGP policy routing, *Computer Networks: The International Journal of Computer and Telecommunications Networking*, **50** (16), pp. 3183–3196.

DOT, (2009) *Economic Impacts of the I-35W Bridge Collapse*, (Department of Employment and Economic Development, Minnesota, USA).
URL:http://www.dot.state.mn.us/i35wbridge/rebuild/municipal-consent/economic-impact.pdf

Emmerson, P., (2007) *Estimating Fuel Consumption in Traffic models*.
URL: www.contram.com/download/forum/2007/Fuel.ppt

Fiksel, J., (2003). Designing Resilient, Sustainable Systems *Environ. Sci. Technol.*, **37** (23), pp. 5330–5339.

Folke, C., Carpenter, S., Elmqvist, T., Gunderson, L., Holling, C. and Walker, B., (2002). Resilience and Sustainable Development: Building

Adaptive Capacity in a World of Transformations, *AMBIO: A Journal of the Human Environment*, **31** (5), pp. 437–440.

Foster, H., (1997). *The Ozymandias Principles: Thirty-one strategies for surviving change*, 1st Ed. (Southdowne Press, Victoria).

Freeman, L.C., (1979). Centrality in Social Networks: Conceptual clarification, *Social Networks* **1**, pp. 215–239.

Freeman, L.C., (2004). *The Development of Social Network Analysis: A Study in the Sociology of Science*. (Emprical Press, Vancouver, Canada).

Gallopin, G.C., (2006). Linkages between vulnerability, resilience, and adaptive capacity, *Global Environmental Change*, **16** (3), pp. 293–303.

Ganguly, A., Nilchiani, R. and Farr, J.V., (2009). Evaluating agility in corporate enterprises, *International Journal of Production Economics*, **118** (2), pp. 410–423.

Garbin, D.A. and Shortle, J.F., (2007). Measuring Resilience in Network-Based Infrastructures, In: McCarthy, J.A. (ed). *Critical Thinking: Moving from Infrastructure Protection to Infrastructure Resilience*.

Goble, G., Fields, H. and Cocchiara, R., (2002) *Resilient infrastructure: Improving your business resilience*, (IBM Global Services). URL: http://www.synergisticonline.com/files/resiliancy.pdf

GOHS, (2010). The Governor's Office of Homeland Security: Transportation Security, Maryland.

Gribble, S.D., (2001). Robustness in Complex Systems', Washington: The University of Washington.

Grote, G., (2004). Uncertainty management at the core of system design, *Annual Reviews in Control*, **28**, pp. 267–274.

Grote, G., (2006). Rules management as source for loose coupling in high-risk systems, *2nd Symposium on Resilience Engineering*. Juan-les-Pins, France.

Haimes, Y., (2006). On the Definition of Vulnerabilities in Measuring Risks to Infrastructures, *Risk analysis; an official publication of the Society for Risk Analysis.*, **26** (2), pp. 293–296.

Haimes, Y.Y., (2004). On the Definition of Vulnerabilities in Measuring Risks to Infrastructures, *Risk Analysis*, p. 26.

Haimes, Y.Y., Crowther, K. and Horowitz, B.M., (2008). Homeland security preparedness: Balancing protection with resilience in emergent systems, *Systems Engineering*, **11** (4), pp. 287–308.

Han, L., (2006) *Measuring "ilities" is a Hopeless Task*, (Rutgers University).
URL: http://www.cs.rutgers.edu/~rmartin/teaching/spring06/cs553/papers/006.pdf

Hastings, D. and McManus, H., (2004). A Framework for Understanding Uncertainty and its Mitigation and Exploitation in Complex Systems, *2004 Engineering Systems Symposium*.

HCM, (2000) *Highway Capacity Manual*, (Transportation Research Board).

Heaslip, K., Louisell, W. and Collura, J., (2009). A Methodology to Evaluate Transportation Resilience for Regional Networks, *88th Annual Meeting of the Transportation Research Board*. Washington, D.C.

Holling, C.S., (1973). 'Resilience and Stability of Ecological Systems'. *Annual Review of Ecology and Systematics*, **4** (1), pp. 1–23.

Holling, C.S., (1996). Engineering Resilience versus Ecological Resilience, *Engineering within ecological constraints*, pp. 31–34.

Horowitz, A.J., (1991) *Delay-Volume Relations for Travel Forecasting: Based on the 1985 Highway Capacity Manual*, (US Department of Transportation, Washington, DC).

HPPM, (2000). *Highway Performance Policy Manual*, (US Department of Transport).

Hudsal, J., (2008). Robustness, flexibility and resilience in the supply chain, *Supply Chain Risk*.
URL: http://www.husdal.com/2008/04/28/robustness-flexibility-and-resilience-in-the-supply-chain/

Hutchinson, A., (2006). Enterprise Resilience Management Blog.
URL: http://enterpriseresilienceblog.typepad.com/enterprise_resilience_man/

IHT, (2006). Asia slowly bounces back from one of region's biggest telecom outages, *International Herald Tribune*. Taipei.
URL: http://www.usatoday.com/news/world/2006-12-28-asia-telecom_x.htm

Isograph, Fault Tree Analysis.
URL: http://www.isograph-software.com/2011/software/reliability-workbench/fault-tree-analysis/

Jackson, S., (2009). *Architechting Resilient Systems*, (John Wiley & Sons Inc., Hoboken, NJ, USA).

Janssen, M.A., (2007). Robustness Trade-offs in Social-Ecological Systems, *International Journal of the Commons*, 1 (1), pp. 43–65.

Johnson-Lenz, P.a.T., (2009). Six Habits of Highly Resilient Organizations, *People and Place*, **1** (2).

Kean, T.H., Hamilton, L.H., Ben-Veniste, R., Kerrey, B., Fielding, F.F., Lehman, J.F., Gorelick, J.S., Roemer, T.J., Gorton, S. and R.Thompson, J., (2010). The 9/11Commission Report.
URL: http://www.9-11commission.gov/report/911Report.pdf

Kema, (2010). *System hardening.*
URL:http://www.kema.com/services/consulting/performance/asset-management/system-hardening.aspx

Kitamura, Y., Lee, Y., Sakiyama, R. and Okamura, K., (2007). Experience with Restoration of Asia Pacific Network Failures from Taiwan Earthquake, *IEICE Trans Commun*, **90** (11), pp. 3095–3103.

Kumar, A. and Motwani, J., (1995). A methodology for assessing time-based competitive advantage of manufacturing firms, *International Journal of Operations & Production Management*, **15** (2), pp. 36–53.

Larson, R., Marks, D., Dahleh, M. and Ilic, M., (2005). *The 3 R's of Critical Energy Networks: Reliability, Robustness and Resilience*, (MIT Energy Research Council).
URL: http://cesf.mit.edu/papers/ThreeRs.pdf

Leveson, N., Nicolas, D., Zipkin, D., Cutcher-Gershenfeld, Carroll, J. and Barrett, B. (2006). *Resilience Engineering: Concepts and Precepts,* eds. Hollnagel, E., Woods, D.D. and Leveson, N., Chapter 8 "Engineering Resilience into a Safety-Critical System," (Ashgate Publishing Company, Burlington, VT), pp. 95–124.

Lingamfelter, S., (2009). Port Security in an All-Hazards World, *The CIP Report, Centre for Infrastructure Protection*, **7** (10).

Little, R.G., (2002). Toward more robust infrastructure: observations on improving the resilience and reliability of critical systems, *Proceedings of the 36th Annual Hawaii International Conference* Hawaii, p. 9.

Madni, A. and Jackson, S., (2009). Towards a Conceptual Framework for Resilience Engineering, *IEEE Systems Journal*, **3** (2), p. 181.

Magee, C.L. and De Weck, O.L., (2002). An attempt at Complex Systems Classification, *ESD-WP-2003-01.02-ESD Internal Symposium*. Massachusetts Institute of Technology Engineering Systems Division.

Mansouri, M., Mostashari, A. and Ganguly, A., (2009a). Evaluating agility in extended enterprise systems: The New York City transportation network case, *1st Annual Global Conference on Systems and Enterprises* Washington, DC.

Mansouri, M., Mostashari, A. and Nilchiani, R., (2009b). A Decision Analysis Framework for Resilience Strategies in Maritime Systems, *IEEE Systems Conference*. Vancouver.

Marra, L.J., (1989). Sharkbite on the SL submarine lightwave cable system: history,causes and resolution, *IEEE Journal of Oceanic Engineering*, **14** (3), pp. 230–237.

Marshall, G. and Chapman, D., (2002). Resilience, Reliability and Redundancy, Copper Development Association.
URL: http://www.copperinfo.co.uk/power-quality/downloads/pqug/41-resilience-reliability-and-redundancy.pdf

Martin Associates (2006). United States Port Sector Economic Impacts.
URL: http://aapa.files.cms-plus.com/PDFs/Port%20Sector%20Economic%20Impacts%20Chart.pdf

MASSDOT, (2007) *Route Traffic Volume Count Listing, Massachusetts*, (Massachusetts Highway Department).
URL: http://www.mhd.state.ma.us/default.asp?pgid=content/traffic01&sid=about#para8

Masse, T., O'Neil, S. and Rollins, J., (2007). *The Department of Homeland Security's Risk Assessment Methodology: Evolution, Issues, and Options for Congress*, (Createspace).

McCarthy, J., (2007). *Critical Thinking: Moving from Infrastructure Protection to Infrastructure Resilience,* eds.McCarthy, J.A., "From Protection to Resilience: Injecting "Moxie" into the Infrastructure Security Continuum," (George Mason University CIP Program Discussion Paper), pp.1–8.

McCormick, J., Aburano, H., Ikenaga, M. and Nakashima, M., (2008). Permissible residual deformation levels for building structures considering both safety and human elements, *The 14th World Conference on Earthquake Engineering*. Beijing, China.

McGregor, (2006). The Cross Harbor Rail Freight Tunnel: A Critical Transportation Project for the New York Region's Future, *National Urban Freight Conference*.

Moody, D.B., (2007). The Need for Resilience at the Corporate Level, In: McCarthy, J.A. (ed). *Critical Thinking: Moving from Infrastructure Protection to Infrastructure Resilience.*

Morlok, E. and Chang, D., (2004). Measuring capacity flexibility of a transportation system, *Transportation research Part A, Policy and Practice*, **38** (6), pp. 405–420.

Moses, J., (2004). *Foundational Issues in Engineering Systems: A framing Paper, Engineering Systems Monograph*, (MIT, Boston). URL: http://esd.mit.edu/symposium/pdfs/day1-2/moses-slides.pdf

Mostahari, A., (2009). Architecting Intelligent/Cognitive Cities, *Global Conference on Systems and Enterprises*, Washington, D.C.

Mostashari, A., (2008). A Primer on Port Infrastructure Operations, Security and Resilience, Stevens Institute of Technology.

Murray-Tuite, P.M., (2006). A comparison of transportation network resilience under simulated system optimum and user equilibrium conditions, *38th conference on Winter simulation*, pp. 1398–1405.

Neill, J., (2006). *What is Psychological Resilience?*. URL: http://wilderdom.com/psychology/resilience/Psychological Resilience.html

Newman, M., (2003). The structure and function of complex networks, *SIAM Review*, **45**, pp.167–256.

Newman, M., (2008). *The New Palgrave Encyclopedia of Economics,* eds. Blume, L.E. and Durlauf, S.N., "Mathematics of networks" (Palgrave Macmillan, Basingstoke).

Nilchiani, R., (2005). Measuring the Value of Space Systems Flexibility: A Comprehensive Six-element Framework, *Department of Aeronautics and Astronautics*. Boston: Massachusetts Institute of Technology, p. 306.

Nilchiani, R. and Hastings, D., (2003). Measuring Flexibility in Design of an Orbital Transportation Network, *AIAA Space 2003 Conference and Exposition*. Long Beach, California.

Niles, S., (2005). *Standardization and Modularity in Network-Critical Physical Infrastructure, Data Centre Solutions.* URL: http://www.apcmedia.com/salestools/VAVR-626VPD_R0_EN.pdf

NIPP, (2009). *National Infrastructure Protection Plan 2009.* (DHS). URL: http://www.dhs.gov/xlibrary/assets/NIPP_Plan.pdf

NJDOT. 'New Jersey Department of Transport'. URL: http://www.state.nj.us/transportation

NRC, (2009) *Sustainable Critical Infrastructure Systems: A Framework for Meeting 21st Century Imperatives*, (The National Academies Press, Washington, DC).

NYSDOT, 'Traffic Data Viewer'.
URL:https://www.nysdot.gov/divisions/engineering/applications/traffic-data-viewer

O'Donnell, A., (2005). Undersea Cable Failure Demonstrates Internet's Vulnerability, *Insurance and Technology*.
URL: http://www.insurancetech.com/showArticle.jhtml?articleID =206901887

O'Rourke, T.D., (2007). Critical Infrastructure, Interdependencies, and Resilience, *The Bridge*, **37** (1), pp. 22–29.

Olivas, R., (2007) *Decision Trees: A Primer for Decision-making Professionals*. URL: http://www.lumenaut.com/download/decision_tree_primer_v5.pdf

Omer, M., Nilchiani, R. and Mostashari, A., (2009). Measuring the Resilience of the Trans-Oceanic Telecommunication Cable System, *IEEE Systems Journal*, **3** (3), pp. 295–303.

Pacine, W. and Callahan, R., (2009). *Resilient International Telecommunications Guidelines for the Financial Sector*. (Financial Services Sector Coordinating Council for Critical Infrastructure Protection and Homeland Security).

Pavard, B., Dugdale, J., Saoud, N.B.-B., Darcy, S. and Salembier, P., (2006). The Design of Robust Socio-Technical Systems, *2nd Symposium on Resilience Engineering*. Juan-les-Pin, France.

Perelman, L.J., (2007). *Critical Thinking: Moving from Infrastructure Protection to Infrastructure Resilience*, eds. McCarthy, J.A., "Shifting Security Paradigms: Toward Resilience," (George Mason University CIP Program Discussion Paper), pp. 23–48.

Pommerening, C., (2007). *Critical Thinking: Moving from Infrastructure Protection to Infrastructure Resilience*, eds. McCarthy, J.A., "Resilience in Organizations and Systems. Background and Trajectories of an Emerging Paradigm," (George Mason University CIP Program Discussion Paper), pp. 9–22.

PSHSB, (2008). *Tech Topic 14: Diversity, Redundancy, and Resilience — in that Order*, (Federal Communications Commission). URL: http://www.fcc.gov/pshs/techtopics/techtopics14.html

Pyle, R., (2006). *Museum tells story of Sept. 11 evacuation by water.* URL: http://www.skyscrapercity.com/showthread.php?t=370063

Reason, J., (2001). The Dimensions of Organisational Resiliene to Operational Hazards, *British Airways Human Factors Conference: Enhancing Operational Integrity.*

Reed, D., Kapur, K. and Christie, R., (2009). Methodology for Assessing the Resilience of Networked Infrastructure, *IEEE Systems Journal*, **3** (2), pp. 174–180.

Resilience-Alliance, (2007). Assessing and managing resilience in social-ecological systems: A practitioners workbook. URL: http://www.resalliance.org/index.php/resilience_assessment

Richards, M.G., Hastings, D.E., Ross, A.M. and Rhodes, D.H., (2007). Design Principles for Survivable System Architecturem, *1st IEEE Systems Conference*. Honolulu, Hawaii, pp. 1–9.

Rinaldi, S., Peerenboom, J. and Kelly, T., (2001). Critical Infrastructure Interdependencies, *IEEE Control Systems Magazine.*

Rodrigue, J.-P., Comtois, C. and Slack, B., (2009). *The Geography of Transport Systems*, (Routeledge, New York).

Rose, A. and Liao, S.-Y., (2005). Modeling Regional Economic Resilience to Disasters: A Computable General Equilibrium Analysis of

Water Service Disruptions, *Journal of Regional Science*, **45** (1), pp. 75–112.

Sadik-Khan, J., (2007). *New York City Bridge Traffic Volumes 2006*, (NYC Department of Transportation). URL: http://www.nyc.gov/html/dot/downloads/pdf/bridgetrafrpt06.pdf

Schulz, A.P. and Fricke, E., (1999). Incorporating flexibility, agility, robustness, and adaptability within the design of integrated systems — key to success?, *18th Digital Avionics Systems Conference*. St Louis, MO.

Scott, D.M., Novak, D., Aultman-Hall, L. and Guo, F., (2005). Network *Robustness Index: A New Method for Identifying Critical Links and Evaluating the Performance of Transportation Networks*, (Centre for Spatial Analysis, McMaster University, Hamilton, Canada).

Sheffi, Y., (2005). *The Resilient Enterprise: Overcoming Vulnerability for Competitive Advantage*, (MIT Press, USA).

Shinozuka, M. and Chang, S.E., (2004) *Modeling Spatial Economic Impacts of Disaster,* eds. Okuyama and Chang S.E., Chapter 14 "Evaluating the Disaster Resilience of Power Networks and Grids," (Springer Verlag, Berlin) pp. 289–310.

Sieger, D.B., Badiru, A.B. and Milatovic, M., (2000). A metric for agility measurement in product development, *IIE Transactions*, **32** (7), pp. 637–645.

Singer, Y., (2006). Dynamic Measure of Network Robustnessm *IEEE 24th Convention of Electrical and Electronics Engineers in Israel*, Eilat, Israel, pp. 366–370.

Skabardonis, A. and Dowling, R., (1997). Improved Speed-Flow Relationships for Planning Applications, *Transportation Research Record, 1572*, pp. 18–23.

Slobin, S., (2009). *Let's Talk About Manhattan,* (Urban Omnibus, New York).
URL: http://urbanomnibus.net/2009/03/lets-talk-about-maps-2/

Sterman, J.D., (2000) *Business Dynamics: Systems Thinking and Modeling for a Complex World,* (Irwin McGraw Hill).

Sugden, A.M., (2001). Resistance and Resilience, *Science,* **293** (5536), p. 1731.

Sussman, J., (2000) *Introduction to Transport Systems,* (Artech House ITS library, Norwood, MA).

Telegeography, (2005). *International VoIP and PSTN Traffic Summary.* URL: www.Telegeography.com

Thorogood, A. and Yetton, P., (2005). Reducing the Technical Complexity and Business Risk of Major Systems Projects, *37th Annual Hawaii International Conference on System Sciences,* Big Island, Hawaii.

Tilahun, N. and Levinson, D., (2007) *I-35W Bridge Collapse: Travel Impacts and Adjustment Strategies,* (University of Minnesota: Nexus Research Group, Minnesota).

Uribe, l., Shigeo Sakai, Cuervo, J., Franklin, H., Mora-Castro, P.G.S., Luis Ferraté, Perez, I., Clark, C. and Bender, S., (1999). *Reducing Vulnerability to Natural Hazards: Lessons Learned from Hurricane Mitch: A Strategy Paper on Environmental Management,* (Consulative Group for the Reconstruction and Transformation of Central America, Stockholm, Sweden).

USDOT, (2008) *National ITS Architecture Version 6.1,* (US Department of Transportation).
URL: http://www.iteris.com/itsarch/

USEPA, (2000) *Emission Facts: Average Annual Emissions and Fuel Consumption for Passenger Cars and Light Trucks*, (US Environmental Protection Agency).
URL: http://www.epa.gov/otaq/consumer/f00013.htm

Walker, B., Gunderson, L., Kinzig, A., Folke, C., Carpenter, S. and Schultz, L., (2006). A Handful of Heuristics and Some Propositions for Understanding Resilience in Social-Ecological Systems, *Ecology and Society*, **11** (1), p.13.

Walker, B., Holling, C.S., Carpenter, S. and Kinzig, A., (2004). Resilience, Adaptability and Transformability in Social–ecological Systems, *Ecology and Society*, **9** (2), p.5.

Wears, R.L. and Perry, S.J., (2008). A Systems Dynamics Representation of Resilience, *3rd Symposium on Resilience Engineering*. Juan-le-Pins, France.

Werner, S.D., (2005). New Developments in Seismic Risk Analysis of Highway Systems, *Research Progress and Accomplishments, 2003-2004*, pp. 221–238.

Westrum, R., (2006). *Resilience Engineering: Concepts and Precepts,* eds. Hollnagel, E., Woods, D.D. and Leveson, N., Chapter 5 "A Typolog of Resilience Situations," (Ashgate Publishing Company, Burlington, VT), pp. 55–65.

Westrum, R., (2006). All Coherence Gone: New Orleans as a Resilience Failure, *Second Resilience Engineering Symposium*. Juan-les-Pins, France.

Whitson, J.C. and Ramirez-Marquez, J.E., (2009). Resilience as a component importance measure in network reliability, *Reliability Engineering and System Safety*, **94**, pp. 1685–1693.

Woods, D. (2005). 'Creating Foresight: Lessons for Enhancing Resilience from Columbia'. In: W. H. Starbuck, W.H. and Farjoun, M. (eds). *Organization at the Limit: Lessons from the Colombia Disaster*, Malden, USA: Blackwell Publishing.

Wreathall, J., (2006). *Resilience Engineering: Concepts and Precepts,* eds. Hollnagel, E., Woods, D.D. and Leveson, N., Chapter 5 "Properties of Resilient Organizations: An Initial View," (Ashgate Publishing Company, Burlington, VT), pp. 275–288.

Wright, E., (2009). Preface to the National Strategy for the Marine Transportation System, *The CIP Report, Centre for Infrastructure Protection,* **7** (10).

Zhang, S. and Dasgupta, P., (2003). Hardened Networks: Incremental Upgrading of the Internet for Attack Resilience, *12th International Conference on Computer Communications and Networks.*

Index